How to AI

How to AI

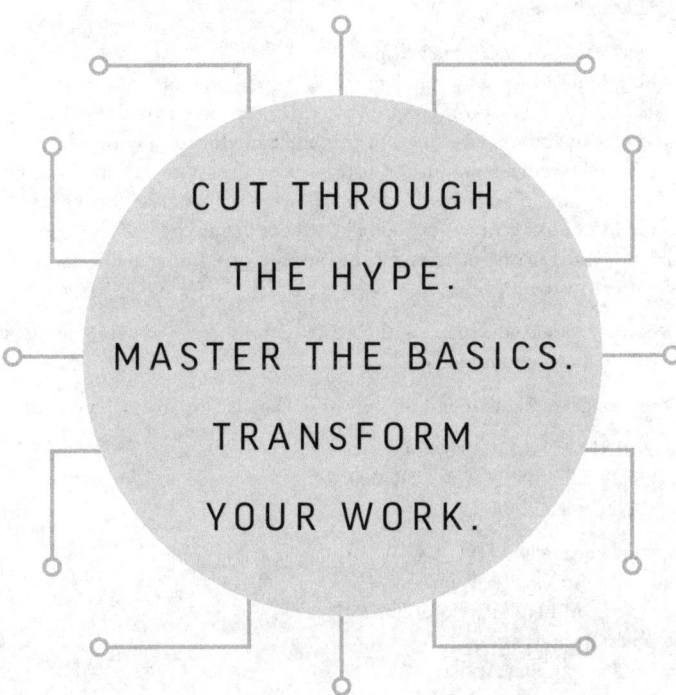

CUT THROUGH
THE HYPE.
MASTER THE BASICS.
TRANSFORM
YOUR WORK.

Christopher Mims

CROWN CURRENCY
New York

CROWN CURRENCY
An imprint of the Crown Publishing Group
A division of Penguin Random House LLC
1745 Broadway
New York, NY 10019
crownpublishing.com
penguinrandomhouse.com

Library of Congress Cataloging-in-Publication Data is available upon request.

Hardcover ISBN 979-8-217-08618-4
International edition ISBN 979-8-217-09006-8
Ebook ISBN 979-8-217-08619-1

Editor: Paul Whitlatch
Editorial assistant: Coalter Palmer
Production editor: Liana Parry Faughnan
Text designer: Aubrey Khan
Production: Christopher Andrus
Copy editor: Lynn Anderson
Proofreaders: Kevin Clift, Chris Fortunato, and Andrea Peabbles
Indexer: J S Editorial, LLC
Publicist: Tara Gilbride
Marketer: Keely Brewer

Manufactured in the United States of America

1st Printing

First Edition

The authorized representative in the EU for product safety and compliance is Penguin Random House Ireland, Morrison Chambers, 32 Nassau Street, Dublin D02 YH68, Ireland, https://eu-contact.penguin.ie.

FOR MARTHA MIMS,
whose love of learning inspires me still

Contents

The Laws of AI

The First Law of AI:
AI is an assistant, not a replacement.

The Second Law of AI:
Experts benefit most from AI.

The Third Law of AI:
AI is a feature, not a product.

The Fourth Law of AI:
To get the most out of AI,
it's essential to make it your own.

The Fifth Law of AI:
Artificial intelligence isn't actually intelligent,
but understanding how it works can unlock its power.

The Sixth Law of AI:
Don't trust it, and always verify its work.

The Seventh Law of AI:
Scaffolding is everything.

The Eighth Law of AI:
Give it your least favorite things to do.

The Ninth Law of AI:
Context is king.

The Tenth Law of AI:
"Garbage in, garbage out" still applies.

The Eleventh Law of AI:
Generative AI enables noncoders to build
useful software that once required a programmer.

The Twelfth Law of AI:
AI makes unstructured data both accessible
and useful in unprecedented ways.

The Thirteenth Law of AI:
AI can create photorealistic images, video, and
audio so convincing that they are rapidly infiltrating
the media we consume—without our knowing it.

The Fourteenth Law of AI:
Generative AI enables previously
unprecedented levels of personalization.

The Fifteenth Law of AI:
"Classic" AI is far more important for the
operation of our world than generative AI.

The Sixteenth Law of AI:
"Classic" predictive AI is brittle
and breaks when big changes occur.

The Seventeenth Law of AI:
AI isn't creative, but it can help you be.

The Eighteenth Law of AI:
AI can't create finished products, but it's
great at quickly generating digital prototypes.

The Nineteenth Law of AI:
Treat AI agents as robots on an assembly line
rather than as assistants.

The Twentieth Law of AI:
When successfully implemented,
AI scales up rote knowledge work.

The Twenty-First Law of AI:
Data is the new rare earths.

The Twenty-Second Law of AI:
Simulation is the next AI frontier.

The Twenty-Third Law of AI:
The most powerful AIs for advancing the frontiers
of human knowledge can help us move faster, but they
cannot replace experimentation in the real world.

The Twenty-Fourth Law of AI:
The field of human endeavor most
transformed by generative AI is coding.

Introduction
The Original Sins of Artificial Intelligence

I t was a mistake to call it artificial intelligence.

I'm not alone in this belief. In November 2022, OpenAI's ChatGPT took the world by storm, but the work that led to it had been quietly building for decades in university laboratories and Silicon Valley office parks. Decades earlier, researchers had anticipated the confusion that calling this stuff artificial intelligence, or AI, would inspire. At a series of meetings in the 1950s, founders of the field we now call AI had a friendly debate about what to name their nascent discipline. Herbert Simon, then a professor at Carnegie Mellon University, suggested the name "complex information processing." Alas, you can see why that never caught on.

But AI itself sure has. As I write this, two and a half years later, half a billion people around the globe are using ChatGPT on a weekly basis. It's the fastest adoption of a new technology in all of history. Yet even as technologists and pundits continue to breathlessly extol the transformative power of this technology, millions of us still don't understand what modern AI really is, how it works, or how to get the most out of it.

I can't blame you for being a little confused. Our world is awash in AI hype. Tech leaders love nothing more than describing their work as revolutionary. This habit is born of equal parts hubris, the cultlike atmosphere of startups, and a need to raise as much money as quickly as possible. Remember the "metaverse"? Sometimes hype really is just that.

AI hype, though, is so big that it's without modern precedent, and for good reason. Chalk it up to the aforementioned "ChatGPT moment." On that day in late November 2022 when OpenAI's AI chatbot became accessible to anyone on the internet, modern generative AI became universally accessible overnight in a way unlike any other new technology in history. With its chatbot, OpenAI bolted a simple, friendly interface onto the front of complex, difficult-to-grasp technology—the "large language model"—making using it as easy as texting with a friend.

Once the AI hype train left the station, it seemed as though nothing could stop it, fueled as it was by a potent mix of breathless news stories and endless social media posts by everyday folks experimenting with AI on their own. By the time the creators of this technology declared that it was potentially so powerful that it might take all our jobs, or in the worst case be an existential threat to all of humanity, we were all primed to pay attention and at least wonder if there was some truth to their pronouncements.

It's easy to forget, or to be blissfully unaware, that discussion about how AI would transform our world predates the ChatGPT moment by decades. AI has been a staple of science fiction since the 1950s, mostly in a way that has primed us to be very nervous about its arrival. By 2015, the powerful and influential head of the World Economic Forum—the annual meeting of which takes place at Davos—coined the term "Fourth Industrial Revolution" to describe the way that AI would lead to changes as big as steam, electricity, and computers had before it.

With the seemingly sudden arrival of generative AI, for some people it felt as though every fantasy about the technology was suddenly being realized. Unfortunately, during the previous decades, many silly ideas had attached themselves to AI that were less than helpful in understanding the reality. We have built machines that are fundamentally different from our own minds, not just in what they're made of but in how they operate, yet we describe them in ways that make them sound as though they're brains made of silicon, every bit as inscrutable and complex as the minds of our fellow humans.

The fuzzy thinking about AI leads to all sorts of wild and mostly unjustified extrapolations. From "AI will take a large portion of the world's jobs" (no, not anytime soon) to "AI could go Skynet and endanger all life on Earth" (yes, but only if we are foolish enough to give it access and powers far beyond what it can requisition on its own).

Amid all this hype and alarm, for some people, the confusion about AI has hardened into skepticism.

Since you picked up this book, I'm going to assume that you're at least curious about AI. Maybe you even use it often, but still you feel overwhelmed by the weekly, even daily dump of new discoveries, announcements, and developments in the field. Perhaps you're turned off by the seemingly scammy, get-rich-quick-with-AI promises of self-promoters on social media. Maybe you fib a bit and pretend—in conversations with colleagues—to be more knowledgeable about AI than you actually are. Or maybe you don't use it at all, but you have a persistent, nagging feeling that you should be, for yourself, your small business, or your team at work. And you worry that if you don't start soon, you might eventually fall behind the technological curve.

Also, let's be real here: Given the way that society always responds to any new labor-saving and productivity-enhancing innovation by demanding ever more of us, we're not far from the day when working without the aid of AI will be like insisting on using a horse and buggy for our morning commute.

Given all the competing narratives about the technology, it's not surprising how many of us still don't know where to begin. Here's the good news: From the perspective of how to use AI to get things done, it's much simpler than you've been led to believe. And depending on your perspective, here's the bad news: AI really will, in time, transform many of the ways we humans do business and live our lives. AI is not the metaverse. It's here to stay, and it's in your best interest to get ahead of where it's going.

Adopting a set of straightforward mental models of what AI is and how it works will allow you not only to navigate but perhaps also to flourish in the next few years or even decades. All sorts of nonexperts, from lawyers and marketers to managers and mom-and-pop construction companies, are using AI tools to augment their work. And for the ones who get it right, AI is making them more productive and their businesses more profitable.

I know because I've been talking to these people for years. For more than a decade, I've been writing a deeply reported weekly column on tech at *The Wall Street Journal*. I've talked to hundreds of people about how they use AI and to just as many people who build or study it, many of them the grandees of the field. After years of such conversations, I've come to realize that it's tricky to say, "Just do it like that other person does!" Teaching the principles of AI is necessarily a bit more complex and benefits from the high-level perspective I've been privileged to gain from peering into the lives and work of so many.

This is because modern AI is so broad in its abilities and is used in ways that are so peculiar to such a wide variety of tasks. It's what historians call a "general-purpose technology," one that impacts countless other activities and industries, such as the automobile or the internet before it. (If you're particularly keen to find out how the kind of AI you're most likely to think of when I say "AI" actually works, recent research on the topic has given us tremendous insight into the subject, and I get into this in chapter 2.)

Plenty of other writers have opined—and a handful have written bestsellers—about the big-picture impact of AI on geopolitics, warfare, medicine, or education. Still more have thrown up get-rich-quick ebooks online. Looking at all of this, I came to realize that something had been missing from the discussion: There was a gap in the universe of conversation about AI and an unmet need for a book that was both pragmatic and thoughtful; a book written for curious people who are skeptical of fads and being sold a bill of goods; a book for ambitious, busy folks who just want to get things done.

· · ·

If you haven't yet engaged deeply with AI, now is the perfect time to start.

In the course of any new technology, there is always a point at which adoption stalls—a chasm between the superearly adopters and the rest of us. We're just hitting this inflection point for AI. It leads to a two-tiered system of advantage in which a fraction of us are reaping the rewards of some fresh development while the rest of us stall, waiting to see whether this new thing is really worth the time and investment.

This book is for people who want to use AI to get things done. That could be done at work, of course, but it's just as likely to occur in other areas of our life. Despite what you might have heard, AI isn't here to squash creativity or usurp the tasks we enjoy doing most; it's here to take over tasks defined as "toil": the repetitive, tedious stuff no one enjoys doing.

On its face, this might seem like a less exciting vision of the abilities of AI than the fever dream of it pushing aside human workers with its superior abilities. But if you're the kind of person who gets excited about getting more out of your team or automating your least favorite parts of your job—or even just someone who wants to better understand how AI might transform the world of work and accelerate innovation—these are heady days.

Throughout this book, you'll encounter five kinds of information. First, the bulk of what you're about to read is stories. I start with stories from individuals and move on to teams and then whole companies. I've taken great care to pick the most accessible and illustrative ones. In many cases, I've gone quite deep into how they use AI, having been granted a degree of access that in my experience as a journalist is rare—and valuable.

The human brain loves narrative—we truly are built for it—and it's the way we structure our memories. Stories are the tools we use to compress our messy, piecemeal understanding of how the world works into a form we can easily recall. If the memory consolidation that happens when you sleep is your brain's compression algorithm, stories are its main product. Every one of the stories in this book illuminates as many general principles of how AI works—and how it can work for all of us—as possible. Stick with me through the narrative ahead, and I'm confident that you'll come away with many durable, useful, memorable lessons about AI.

Second, this book is full of what I call the "Laws of AI." These aren't scientific laws but are more like the rules of thumb that engineers rely on when designing things. They're applicable in most but not all situations. We don't always know why these rules work, as our understanding of how AI works—that is, the science of AI—is still evolving. But look, if the Wright brothers didn't need supercomputers and models of fluid dynamics to create wings that made possible the first powered flight, rules of thumb about the behavior of AI that work but that are incompletely understood are good enough as well.

Third, I'm going to give you a running glossary of new terms. This isn't just because I adore and am a lifelong collector of new words. (Did you know that "sesquipedalian" is the adjective for an excessively long word?) Unnecessary jargon is often used by experts in a field to exclude outsiders. But I promise that I will limit my use of it to genuinely new and useful concepts. AI is full of these, and every new word in this field is an opportunity to get a handle on a concept that can grant you new skills, make you sound smart in a job interview, or just give you a new way to look at the world.

Fourth, I'm going to give you the occasional aside on the history of AI. "How did we get here?" is a surprisingly helpful question to ask of modern AI—more helpful, I would argue, than excessively detailed recitations of its inner workings. Retracing the history of the development of AI is another way to make its clockwork mathematical guts more accessible and memorable, by turning them into another kind of story.

Finally, at the end of every chapter, I'm going to sum up everything you just learned with two statements and a provocation. I'm going to tell you, in the most succinct and direct way I know how, what to know about what you just read. Then, to put it into context, I'm going to tell you how to think about it. And I'll close with what questions to ask when you're applying that knowledge to the real world.

To begin, we'll tackle the most basic building blocks of everyday, useful AI and how they make up the systems used by individuals tackling straightforward and narrow tasks. Part II goes into how AI can be used by teams for more complicated and ambitious work. And part III takes us out of today's bubble of hype for the kinds of AI you're most likely to be familiar with and into the realm of companies applying it in ways that few people know about—and more of us should.

Chapter by chapter, brick by conceptual brick, we'll build up our understanding of AI and its applications. By the end of this book, we'll be in the rarefied air of those working at the cutting edge of AI. You'll know what AI is good at and what it isn't—yet. You'll have a sense of the breadth of AI software and services that people are turning to now to level up their work. My hope is that by that point, your confidence in the subject, bolstered by your own experiments with AI, will be at a point where you'll feel inspired to think about applying it to areas of human endeavor in which only you—the expert in your field, the protagonist of your own journey—would think to do so.

· · ·

Remember my beef with the term *AI*?

In the pages that follow, I will succumb to convention and call AI by its generally accepted name. But in my own mind, I think of it as "simulated intelligence," and perhaps you should, too. Simulated intelligence reminds us that while AI can sometimes fool us into thinking it's intelligent in the same ways that we are, at a fundamental level we're dealing with something very different from us. It emphasizes just how alien it is, compared to ourselves, our pets, even the things that creep and crawl on this earth and that I spent the early part of my twenties investigating during my brief stint as an invertebrate neuroscientist in the lab of an MIT-trained electrical engineer.

This much is true about the AI hype: We are at the dawn of a new age. AI is truly a new general-purpose technology. It's one that will be useful, or at least impactful, in every field of human endeavor. AI is akin to other technologies that transformed whole societies, such as the steam engine, the automobile, the PC, and the internet. As in technological transitions past, those who can understand and make the most of these developments will have considerable advantages, economic and otherwise, compared to those who do not.

So what are we waiting for? Let's dive in.

Part I

AI FOR INDIVIDUALS

1

DON'T PANIC

Kim Jones Penepacker is a lawyer in Dallas, Texas, who often spends the better part of her workday in the company of AI. She's not just using AI; she's working alongside it. It monitors her constantly and gives her feedback on her job performance.

That might sound dystopian, even Orwellian, but Kim wouldn't have it any other way. And I'm willing to bet that were you in her shoes, you'd feel the same. Or at least I hope so, because whatever your job may be, it's likely that your experience of work will someday resemble hers.

In the not-too-distant future, almost all of us will do our work both better and faster as a result of AI. There will be holdouts, people who remain convinced that the usurpation of their cognitive labors by AI will compromise the quality of their work or could lead to their own irrelevance. But for most of us, delegating to AI the parts of our jobs that are tedious and time consuming will be liberating.

Kim is a character—maybe even a bit of a caricature. She's a personal injury lawyer at Aulsbrook Car & Truck Wreck Injury Lawyers, which bills itself as "The Home of the Texas Law Dog." (The "law dog" in question is the firm's founder, Matthew E. Aulsbrook, who never appears in court without his trademark jet-black Stetson cowboy hat.) Kim got her law degree at Baylor, a

Christian university in central Texas, met her husband when volunteering at an animal shelter, dotes on her two dogs, and is the brainy, slightly nerdy counterpoint to Matthew's twangy braggadocio.

On its face, using AI in the legal field feels like a recipe for disaster. And Kim is well aware of the pitfalls. One of the first things she told me when we talked about her work was how her approach to using AI was *nothing* like the very public disasters faced by certain other attorneys who have tried to cut corners by using AI.

Ever since the debut of ChatGPT, less-than-careful attorneys have gotten into trouble for attempting to use it to write legal briefs, leading to citations of made-up cases, nonsense legal reasoning, and even judges issuing sanctions. In one infamous case, a New York judge fined a pair of lawyers $5,000 for using ChatGPT to write a brief that included a half-dozen fictitious cases, for making "false and misleading statements to the court." Their response, which would be laughable if it wasn't typical of the way many Americans think modern AI works, was that they had "made a good faith mistake in failing to believe that a piece of technology could be making up cases out of whole cloth."

People who use AI well know you can't simply ask AI to do your job for you, whether in law or any other field. Yet there are many, many tasks in which AI can help lawyers—as long as they use it appropriately. From legal discovery, in which varieties of AI that allow for new kinds of fuzzy or "semantic" searches are tremendously helpful, to the *appropriate* use of AI in writing briefs, it's possible that no field will be more thoroughly transformed by AI in the coming years than the law.

Taking depositions is a prime example. It's part of the research and fact-gathering portion of a legal confrontation, and it happens before two parties settle or go to trial. A deposition usually takes place in an office or over Zoom and is a kind of structured interview, a more sedate version of the questioning of a witness we've all seen in courtroom dramas.

For almost all of history, a deposition required nothing more technologically sophisticated than pen and paper. Lawyers would come up with a list of questions relevant to the case and try to pin down the person they were deposing in the hope that they would say things that would help their client's case. Lying in a deposition is perjury, so this process isn't about tricking someone so much as it's about asking direct questions and getting clear answers.

The pre-AI version of this process required the kind of mental gymnastics that would lead experienced lawyers to fail to get what they needed out of the person they were deposing. Simultaneously, they had to listen closely to what someone was *actually* saying as it might be rendered in a transcript, improvise appropriate follow-up questions, and all the while verify that they were getting what they needed out of the interview.

This is where AI comes in. Kim uses an AI "copilot" from the legal tech startup Filevine. Before the deposition, she uploads a list of all of her questions. During the deposition, Filevine's copilot records the conversation and transcribes it in real time. This is itself a minor miracle of AI technology, but not a new one. AI transcription systems have existed for decades but have only in recent years come close to the accuracy of an experienced human who is familiar with the specialized vocabulary of a field.

As the deposition proceeds, Filevine's copilot feeds the transcript to a large language model—the same thing that powers cutting-edge chatbots such as the ones behind OpenAI's ChatGPT, Anthropic's Claude, Google's Gemini, and the like. That model has been primed with plain-English written instructions. Those instructions tell the model to compare all of Kim's questions to the transcript of the deposition as the deposition is happening.

This is where the magic of modern AI kicks in. Unlike a conversation with a chatbot, which plods along at a pace dictated by a human's ability to read and respond, this is a conversation between an AI agent and itself. And the information being fed to the AI agent and compared, over and over again, to Kim's initial list of deposition questions is the transcript of the conversation between two humans. Filevine's AI is, in short, tasked with completing a task on its own. That task is relatively simple for a human but until quite recently was utterly impossible for a machine: to determine whether or not Kim has gotten sufficiently clear answers to all the questions she brought to the deposition.

In some ways, the deposition AI copilot is worse than a human at this task. It can be pedantic, simplistic, too literal; its judgment isn't always great. But even if it has its limitations, its mind doesn't wander and it can catch things that Kim would otherwise miss.

"We are attorneys, we're biased," said Kim, recalling a deposition she had been conducting for a case following a car accident. "Broadly, my goal was, I wanted this defendant to say my client did not cause the crash." She got the defendant to admit that her client had never left their lane, and in her mind, that was the answer she needed. But the deposition AI copilot wasn't satisfied. It stubbornly refused to check off the question she'd entered into it before the deposition had begun: Was her client *not* responsible for the crash? "Logically, I know when someone says that my client never left their lane, then the defendant must have left their lane and caused the crash. But the deposition copilot said that while I did get them to admit they changed lanes, I didn't complete the goal."

This is the kind of subtlety that's easy to miss, especially when an attorney is working by themselves and facing a reluctant witness. Were one present, a second attorney on Kim's side might catch the moment a defendant answers a question in a way that's unsatisfactory. But in this case, the AI *is* that second attorney. It's not perfect and it can't do her job for her, but it gives Kim a leg up on the competition.

Kim said that having a deposition copilot listen in on her interviews and automatically flag when she hasn't met her goals means that she's that much more likely to get the information she needs to leverage a better deal in a settlement—or to get exactly the testimony she needs to win if the case goes to trial. She uses it almost every time she does a deposition. The first time we talked, that meant she'd used it every day the week before, a mark of how it had become indispensable to her. "I feel like a lot of lawyers are looking at AI as 'How can it do my job for me?' and not 'How can I enhance my job performance with it?'" she said. "At the end of the day, it's a tool. As exciting as AI is, using it to enhance what you are already doing is key for me."

Her explanation is a perfect segue to our First Law of AI; even the most powerful of today's AI chatbots are at best assistants for humans—not replacements.

The First Law of AI:
AI is an assistant, not a replacement.

You might object that AI is becoming smarter every day. And aren't AI agents able to replace humans in some jobs, for example, customer service?

It's true that AI can take over and nearly fully automate some simple, repetitive, well-defined tasks. There are, most assuredly, some categories of back-office jobs that might disappear entirely, and soon, such as processing invoices. But the human jobs that AI might take over completely are for the foreseeable future the kinds of tedious and borderline mindless jobs that companies outsourced long ago, and the potential further impact of AI on those jobs in advanced economies such as the United States is low. This is not to say that someone who teams up with AI won't replace others who aren't using it. For some jobs, this might even mean one person doing the work of several unaided humans.

That's a topic we'll explore in depth in subsequent chapters, in the context of this important nuance of modern AI: The insurmountable limitations of today's AI systems mean that they almost always require, at minimum, human supervision. And in the overwhelming majority of cases, AIs are merely tools requiring that we actively wield them. Power tools may have been one of the defining innovations of the Industrial Revolution, but no one would call the steam drill a robot, much less an autonomous one.

From the First Law of AI follows a second, which you may find surprising: Most of the time, AI helps the expert more than the amateur. This flies in the face of our gut instincts about AI, which derive from our misunderstanding of what it is.

Logically, it may strike you as sensible—if we believe that AI is in any meaningful sense of the word smarter than we are—that someone who isn't practiced in a field could leverage AI to perform as well as an expert does. But that simply isn't the case. Because AI is merely a tool, in most cases it's only as good as the person who wields it.

Ethan Mollick, a professor at the Wharton School who is an obsessive documenter of the ever-evolving abilities and limitations of AI, has pointed out in his writing and our conversations that the more you know about a field, the more you can get out of today's cutting-edge AI. That's because experts, whether they're coders or MDs, are able to ask AIs better questions and then continue following up with more prompts, pushing the AI ever deeper into their databases of knowledge. They're also—and this is critical—better able to evaluate an AI's responses and recognize when the AI gets something wrong.

While the way in which AI can help experts more than amateurs may contradict our intuition, it aligns with even the most cursory examination of the history of automation and the technologies that enable it. In my first book, on the automation of the world's supply chains, I exhaustively documented the ways in which automation has taken over more and more of the most menial physical tasks—sorting packages, moving boxes, even driving trucks—and left behind only the things that humans are best at. Automation, as ever, needs us even more than we need it.

The Second Law of AI:
Experts benefit most from AI.

One of the defining features of Filevine's deposition copilot is that under the hood, there's less to differentiate it from other AIs than you might think.

This is the secret of the overwhelming majority of today's AI services: They're all using the same handful of AI "minds." Whether you're talking to an AI when ordering at the drive-through of a fast-food restaurant, your therapist is using AI to summarize their notes from your latest session, or your lawyer is using Filevine's deposition copilot, they're all running on OpenAI's ChatGPT, Anthropic's Claude, Google's Gemini, xAI's Grok, Amazon's Nova, or an open-source model from Meta, Mistral, or DeepSeek. Part of the reason they're using these "frontier" models, aside from the fact that they are the best, is that they're also increasingly interchangeable. There's even evidence that as models become more capable, their outputs converge on the same responses.

The net result of all of these forces is that those who build AI apps are, as they are fond of telling me, "model agnostic." This is a point of pride for them, because it means that if one model advances faster or proves to be better at a particular task, they can easily swap one out for another.

Just as often, the companies building AI apps such as Filevine's deposition copilot are using a variety of AI models on the back end, handing tasks to whichever is cheapest or most capable. Scratch the surface of a modern AI startup, and the "brain" its system is running on is likely to be toggling between ChatGPT and its many competitors. We live in an age in which, as OpenAI CEO Sam Altman memorably put it, intelligence is becoming too cheap to meter.

The continually falling price of access to today's AIs and the way the companies building them keep pace with one another in terms of features and abilities mean that even the most sophisticated AI models are becoming commodities. The definition of a commodity is, after all, that it's interchangeable, the way one barrel of oil or bushel of wheat is as good as any other.

Perhaps the most important result of the commodification of generative AI is that the future of how most of us interact with it will be not with chatbots but applications. The main reason for this is that open-ended conversations with AI, in which it's up to the skill of the user to make these enormously capable—but also complex—systems do their best is not the kind of user interface that any but AI's most enthusiastic early adopters will accept. (It's no coincidence that those early adopters are mostly programmers or people with a programming background who are accustomed to typing long strings of text into machines and endlessly tweaking those prompts to get systems to behave.) Applications, on the other hand, are already a familiar interface for working with computers, the conventions of which have evolved to meet our needs and foibles. What's more, combining AI with conventional software, a process I'll get into in chapter 3, is where the real magic happens in terms of making AI both accessible and useful.

To put it another way, in the future, AI will be a feature and not a product. For many of us, it will be invisible, wrapped up deep in the code of services and applications that we already find familiar.

The Third Law of AI:
AI is a feature, not a product.

Today, the fact that Kim's deposition copilot has AI under the hood feels novel—yes, even a touch revolutionary. But it won't feel that way for long. In the future, the inclusion of AI in a legal tool such as this will be as unremarkable as a bookkeeper using the "Formulas" tab on Microsoft Excel. The definition of technology, I have learned from many years of covering it, is whatever we are still coming to grips with. Once its evolution has slowed enough for us to take it for granted, it's merely infrastructure.

To get the most out of AI is, more than anything, a matter of finding the software tools that will integrate it most seamlessly and leverage it to accomplish things that no other app or service can. It's not very sexy to say this, but it's true: Using AI well turns out to be the old problem of how to evaluate new software and IT systems. The good—and exciting—news is that these systems create a huge variety of new capabilities, almost low-key superpowers, that can, depending on your role, fundamentally change not just how you do your job but what that job is.

We'll get into that in the next chapter.

TERMS

Artificial intelligence: A misnomer. Early architects of the field proposed calling it "complex information processing."

General-purpose technology: A foundational technology with broad applications, such as the steam engine, telecommunications—or AI.

Copilot: An AI agent that is always on in the background, monitoring what you do and offering assistance when appropriate.

Agent: A kind of AI that has some ability to perform at least part of a task on its own.

ChatGPT, Claude, Gemini, Llama, Le Chat: Chatbot interfaces of frontier AI models from OpenAI, Anthropic, Google, Meta, and Mistral.

Frontier model: The most capable AI models available today; all are trained at enormous expense, usually for more than $100 million apiece, on gigantic clusters of microchips designed solely to create AIs.

Model agnostic: A fancy way to say that the software someone is trying to sell you is based on a generic AI model that could be swapped out for any other AI model without your even noticing.

SUMMARY
What to Know
AIs are assistants in the workplace, not replacements for workers, and will help experts more than amateurs. In the future, AI will almost always be a feature of the tools we use, rather than a product in itself.

How to Think About It
Figuring out how to get the most out of AI means doing the same thing everyone who uses information technology has been doing for decades: identifying and experimenting with software and services while being agnostic about the technology they use to deliver a desired result.

What Questions to Ask
When the makers of a tool claim it has new abilities thanks to the addition of AI, what exactly are they? How do they enhance the work

someone is already doing? Can these abilities be delivered consistently? If not, what amount of human monitoring, attention, or intervention is required? Will the addition of AI to this tool actually increase a person's productivity in a *measurable* way, or is the focus on improving the quality of the work it helps to accomplish? If the latter, who is evaluating the change in quality of the work, and are their judgments made without reference to the fact that the work was accomplished with the help of AI?

2

KEEP CALM
AND EMBRACE AI

Leanne Shelton had a problem common to many in her field: Work was drying up on account of her clients turning to AIs such as ChatGPT. A freelance copywriter in a suburb of Sydney, Australia, Leanne is smart, quick, enthusiastic, and voluble—exactly the kind of communicator you'd want to convey your company's message. Yet a growing number of the companies and individuals who used to rely on her were opting to use AI to generate copy. And some were turning to writers who charged less on account of using AI to boost their productivity.

Stories such as Leanne's can seem idiosyncratic. Is job loss due to AI really a widespread issue, or is this narrative exaggerated by the media, with its bias for negative, eye-catching stories? The answer, as always, lies in the data. Ever since the debut of ChatGPT in November 2022, a steady flow of research has backed up the idea that, given the choice, companies will use AI to perform low-level tasks they used to farm out to freelancers and junior employees.

The impact of AI on the demand for various sorts of work varies a great deal by field and by the complexity of the task. One 2024 study by the freelance job posting site Upwork found that job postings on the site for "low-value" writing had plummeted by nearly 20 percent in the first two years after ChatGPT's debut. Another study found a drop of 17 percent in jobs for image creation. A third found a drop in demand for low-level coding tasks.

It's a tale I've heard from many freelancers who have lost work to AI and seen their incomes crater as a result. Jennifer Kelly, a sixty-two-year-old freelance copywriter in New Hampshire, told me that she pitied any young people trying to enter her field. "We'll be okay, our house is paid for and I can get Social Security," she said but then added wistfully, "I thought I'd probably work till I was seventy."

And it's not just writers. AI image-generating services have come for the work of concept artists, whose traditional role is sketching ideas for the look of characters and scenes in movies and television series. Using increasingly sophisticated AI image generators that require only a text prompt—or a freelancer skilled at prompting them—more and more producers, who are facing pressure to cut costs, have disposed of human concept artists. Reid Southen, a twentysomething concept artist in LA who had previously worked on *The Matrix Resurrections* and the Marvel film *Blue Beetle,* told me that in 2023 his income had dropped to half what it would be in a typical year—and that it was even worse than in 2020, when pandemic shutdowns had frozen his entire industry. Some of this is attributable to bigger forces in his industry, but Southen's specialty—creating art that will never appear in films or television but that is essential for the brainstorming phase of production—has, like other forms of preproduction work, been disrupted by generative AI.

But for those determined to coexist with AI, it's not all bad news. As her income from traditional copywriting began to ebb, Leanne decided to start playing with the very tools that threatened her livelihood. She had natural advantages: irrepressible optimism and a disposition as sunny as the New South Wales coast near her home. While others in her industry have shied away from technology they see as a threat, she decided she had no choice but to embrace it.

When I first spoke to her in early 2024, her focus was on using AI to make herself more productive. That made sense, since fierce competition among the companies behind the AI chatbots she was testing meant that they were all rapidly becoming both more capable and cheaper—a trend that has only accelerated. The free versions of today's chatbots are already far better than what Leanne started with in 2023, part of a trend that OpenAI CEO Sam Altman has called "intelligence too cheap to meter."

Most people know about ChatGPT, which is the Kleenex or Xerox of the field, the product that has become synonymous with the category. But there are a shocking number of other companies in an arms race to build so-called frontier or foundation models, which is jargon for the biggest, most capable AIs out there.

Despite the fact that training these kinds of frontier models costs upward of $100 million, they have proliferated. Options include Claude, from the startup Anthropic; Gemini, by Google; and Le Chat—get it?—from Mistral, a company based in Paris. Then there's DeepSeek, the Chinese upstart that rocked the AI world in early 2025; Microsoft Copilot, which was built in collaboration with OpenAI but isn't the same thing as ChatGPT; Meta's Meta AI, based on the company's Llama models; OLMo, from the not-for-profit Allen Institute for AI; and Amazon's Nova. There are also quite a few frontier models from Chinese companies, from both startups and the usual Chinese tech giants, including Alibaba, Baidu, and Tencent. Finally, there's Apple Intelligence, which, though lacking in capabilities compared to its competitors, has the advantage of being free.

Then there are the endless apps and services that are basically just app- or web-based interfaces that provide access to these frontier models and, by providing additional material for the AI in a consistent but largely invisible way, may modify their behavior in meaningful ways. These are built by startups with far fewer resources than the big AI labs that produce foundation models, but their creators have some idea about a service they think they can build with them. (As I outlined in the previous chapter, these services are the way most people will use and encounter AI in the future.)

If you think about it, it's pretty funny that these gigantic tech companies and improbably well funded startups have spent, collectively, tens of billions of dollars to build AI models that do more or less the same thing and continue to burn cash as though there couldn't possibly be a better use for it. In part, this is because many company executives have convinced themselves—and their backers—that they're in a race to build a human-level intelligence, known as artificial general intelligence, or AGI.

Spoiler alert: Despite what you may have heard, AGI isn't coming anytime soon—but more on that later. This is an industry that is *definitely* headed for consolidation and some spectacular flameouts, the same way as in the 1990s dot-com bust, when countless specialist retailers and online services closed shop and were replaced by a handful of giant winners, such as Google and Amazon.

It's the unbelievable largesse of these competing AI services and their investors (thanks to Saudi Arabia's Public Investment Fund!) that has made possible the rapid evolution of Leanne's use of ChatGPT and its competitors. In early 2025, a year into her transformation from freelance copywriter to AI-using freelance copywriter, I spoke with her a second time. She had some surprising news: She was basically done being a copywriter, even with the help of AI. By that time, she had become someone who coached others on how to use AI, including how to use it to write advertising and marketing copy for themselves. The results of her clients' AI-generated efforts were not, she took pains to emphasize, the kind of anonymous, empty-headed dreck that AI content generation services typically produce. "So many AI tools are crap," she emphasized.

Her secret to getting AI to help her produce better work, faster? Making AI her own. "I wrote an article on Tuesday," she said. "It took me an hour. It was eighty-nine percent AI, but it sounds like me."

While many writers favor the writing voice of Anthropic's Claude, Leanne favors ChatGPT for the simple reason that it "just knows my voice so well." The reason it does is that she's been using it for two years. You see, today's AI chatbots have a primitive form of memory. The longer you use them, the better they become at adapting themselves to you. Just as important, knowing how to augment this memory by feeding them samples of the kind of work you want them to draw on and produce can allow you to further customize them to sound like you or deliver content formatted in ways you prefer.

While it's not possible to teach today's AI chatbots things the same way we teach ourselves, a child, or a pet, we can modify their outputs by feeding them the right information. But there are limits to how well the memory of today's AI chatbots works, and understanding the nature of those limitations is key to getting the most out of them. This process of tuning an AI's outputs is how we make them our own and is essential to getting these systems to do useful work. That's our next law.

The Fourth Law of AI:
To get the most out of AI,
it's essential to make it your own.

To fully unpack how one copywriter in a sun-drenched corner of New South Wales completely changed her career in the span of twelve months by becoming really good at using AI chatbots—

and adapting them to her needs, we must embark upon the most important detour in this book. It'll be our first step in building for ourselves a functional, high-level understanding of how today's generative AIs actually work.

There will be no math or quizzes. There will be a minimum of jargon. And we're going to go about this in a way that is probably unfamiliar to you—even if you've already studied how today's generative AIs work. Rather than try to describe how today's AIs work from the ground—or the equation—up, we're going to go from the top down. We're going to start at the level of abstraction that is most relevant to doing real work with them.

This is a technique I learned from my stint as a neuroscientist. In the antediluvian era known as the turn of the last millennium, I was an undergraduate in an unusually broad program at Emory University in Atlanta, Georgia, called Neuroscience and Behavioral Biology. It combined courses in basic neuroscience—I still remember doing the math required to model the behavior of individual neurons—with ones in animal behavior, human psychology, and biological anthropology. Later, I spent a couple of years as a working scientist in an invertebrate neuroscience lab at another university in Atlanta. That lab focused, to what I now realize was an archaic and unusual degree, on the low-level, nitty-gritty mechanics of how living nervous systems work.

In that windowless, electrically shielded basement, I spent countless hours poking the still living neurons of crayfish, which are blessed with a large, well-defined neuron running the length of their tails, with impossibly tiny glass electrodes. I stimulated those neurons for hours, spritzed them with neurotransmitters to modify their behavior, and watched their responses on an honest-to-goodness oscilloscope, as if it were still the 1950s.

What I learned from the tender, formative years I spent learning about and doing research on nervous systems at various levels of abstraction, from individual molecules all the way up to whole behaving animals, can be summed up in a single sentence: Neuro-science is a pretty shit way to try to understand the human mind. The problem isn't the science, which is excellent; it's the complexity. If you want to know why an animal or person did a thing, you are never in a million years going to be able to reconstruct every impulse of every nerve that inspired that action, thought, or utterance. Even if you could capture a full picture of all of the neural processing that led to a behavior, our human minds simply don't have the capacity to grasp it.

Fortunately, there's an alternate way to understand why people do the things they do, and it works equally well for understanding why modern AIs do the things they do: cognitive psychology. In humans, cognitive psychology is the study of how our minds work, at a level of abstraction that's just below conventional psychology. How do memory and attention work, and what is their interplay? How does language inform our view of the world? What are the nearly two hundred biases that distort and inform our decision making? These are all questions asked by cognitive psychologists.

The nascent field of cognitive psychology, but applied to AI, is known as "machine psychology." The rest of this book will, in one way or another, touch on this field. Whereas most explanations of how AI works start somewhere down in its cockles, rooting about in the untangleable spaghetti of artificial neural networks, "attention heads," backpropagation, hidden layers, and all the other Rube Goldberg miscellany of AI's mathematical underpinnings, we're going to start at the top. In the spirit of the pioneers of psychology—Sigmund Freud, Jean Piaget, B. F. Skinner—we will begin with what we can easily observe about AI and add to that the research of computer scientists who are concocting novel tools to poke at it. Later, we will go deeper into the workings of AI, one layer at a time but never beyond the point at which our spelunking becomes esoteric or distracting.

In that spirit, here are the things you need to know about generative AI to understand how to emulate Leanne and make it able to write whatever you like—emails, documents, even apologies—in ways that are close to how you yourself would.

First, there's what today's generative AIs actually are. They aren't—and I cannot stress this enough—intelligent in any meaningful sense of the word. The most simplistic definition of how they work is that, given a series of words, they predict the next most likely word. The chat interface of an AI chatbot is really just a clever design choice laid atop this basic fact. When you interact with the large language models that underpin today's AI chatbots—and countless other AI tools—what you're really doing is, in essence, writing a collaborative story with them.

Given such a simple mechanism, how on earth can today's large language models predict the next word in a sequence in a way that allows them to interact with us in a way that *appears* intelligent? The facile answer favored by people whose billion-dollar fortunes depend on this being true is that in some sense these models *are* intelligent. This is very convenient for startup founders seeking unheard-of amounts of investment to build AI supercomputers, as it implies that if investors just give them enough billions, their silicon pets will soon demonstrate that they are in fact as intelligent as we are in ways that are irrefutable.

HOW MODERN AIs WORK

There is and will continue to be much debate about the capabilities of today's AIs. It's made all the messier by our imprecise definitions of intelligence in our own and other species. There is, fortunately, an even simpler question we can ask about today's AIs, which is: Are they genuinely capable of reasoning?

The short answer, from those who study this question deeply and aren't trying to sell us anything, is that mounting evidence points to a truly bizarre underlying mechanism for today's large language models, one significantly different from the way that humans and even many animals appear to model and make decisions about the world. Best of all, this mechanism helps explain a number of quirks of the behavior of today's AIs.

Today's AIs simulate intelligence by learning impossibly long lists of rules of thumb, which they then call upon to generate new content. (In the case of large language models, what they're generating is the next word in a document or chat.)

Researchers call this way of working a "bag of heuristics." *Heuristic* is a fancy word for a rule of thumb—and using a long list of them to solve a task or predict the next word in a sequence is *very* different from what the hypers of today's AI think those AIs are doing. Many in the field of AI—and I'm talking about some of the biggest and most recognizable names in the field, people who can raise billions of dollars for new startups just by putting out their hand—think that AI is thinking as people do, more or less. By this logic, if only we make AIs bigger and cram ever more information into them, they will become superhuman in their abilities, just as a person would who had the capacity to read and remember everything people have ever generated and put onto the internet.

The "bag of heuristics" way of working for today's AIs applies to not just large language models but all of the kinds of AIs that are based on the same underlying collection of algorithms. This underlying model is called a *transformer.* Transformers can be applied to a dizzying array of fields and types of data, from mathematics and genetics to the movements of robots and autonomous vehicles.

While transformer models can learn from many different kinds of data—and with minimal human intervention—it's easy to see why their results are often described as brittle. Many such models exhibit unpredictable behaviors and, worse yet, are unpredictably unpredictable. That is, you rarely know in what circumstances they will break and generate a nonsense response until they do. This is annoying in a chatbot and disastrous in a self-driving car. No matter how large the bag of heuristics may be, it's apparent that today's AI models have trouble coping with situations that fall outside the data they've used to come up with those rules of thumb in the first place.

This is the point at which I must regretfully inform you that this book is as free of AI hype as I've been able to make it. This does not mean that AI won't transform all our lives—just as the internet, mobile phones, the automobile, and Xanax have. It just means that AI is a powerful but limited tool, one that is perhaps unusually tricky to get right.

The Fifth Law of AI:
Artificial intelligence isn't actually intelligent, but understanding how it works can unlock its power.

Back to memory and AI. The fact that today's AIs are "bags of heuristics" does not on its own suggest why they have such a limited ability to remember things that we, their end users, tell them. After all, couldn't the rules of thumb that make up their "brains" be updated to reflect new information, just as the human brain regularly reconfigures its neurons into new networks that encode fresh memories and behavior patterns?

To understand why Leanne has had to spend considerable time and effort feeding writing samples and information about herself to her AI in order to get it to write in her style, you have to understand one other important fact about large language models: Unlike a human or an animal, even today's most cutting-edge AIs are fixed things. They are trained on vast quantities of information in giant AI-making factories called data centers. OpenAI doesn't like to give out exact numbers, but it's been estimated that it trained its GPT-3 model on about 500 billion words. GPT-4 was trained on approximately 10 *trillion* words.

Once that training is done, a model is fully baked. Its tendencies can be tuned in various ways, but again, that all happens at the AI factory. Once the average person is interacting with one of these systems, all of the endless connections among its various digital neurons, called weights, are set in stone. I have often found that the adage "You can't teach an old dog new tricks" isn't true—but it is absolutely true of AIs.

The only way we, the typical end users, can modify the behavior of an AI is by feeding it information for it to "think about" while it's running for us. When an AI model is running for us, it's called inference, and it's distinct from the formative training it underwent at the data center.

All language models have what's known as a "context window" into which is crammed the entirety of the current conversation we're having with that AI, plus the contents of any documents or web pages we've handed to it, plus whatever is in the stable but modifiable "memory" of that AI chatbot. If you think of an AI's context window as its short-term memory, holding on to all of that at once is quite a feat.

But here's the tricky bit. For reasons that would require more math to describe than I've promised myself I would put in this book, for every tenfold increase in the number of words you give an AI chatbot, the number of mathematical operations it must perform to "think" about those words increases by a factor of about 100. (For the math nerds: The increase is quadratic, so really the increase is about 110.)

You can see how this can quickly get out of hand. When it comes to simple prompts, today's AI chatbots have no trouble generating responses faster than any person can read them. But longer conversations and more complicated tasks make demands

on the computers running them—in the remote data centers that
make up the cloud—that are far in excess of what's required to,
say, do a Google search or stream a movie. If you've heard about
the insatiable demands of today's AIs, including Amazon buying
up the capacity of an entire nuclear power plant and Microsoft
restarting a nuclear reactor at Three Mile Island to power a new
data center, this is in part what all that is about.

The makers of modern AIs solve the problem of their runaway
demand for computing by limiting how much they have to remember at any one time. If you're a developer and willing to pay
for more computing power, you can get some really gigantic context windows; Google's Gemini, for example, has an enormous
context window of up to 1 million "tokens," where each token
corresponds to roughly one word. Other services typically limit
users to about a tenth of that. Every AI company is employing
every trick in the book, from using new and more efficient hardware to offering smaller and less powerful AI models, to try to
keep a lid on the cost of the servers and data centers they have to
buy and the electricity it takes to run them.

This explains why, when Leanne asks her chatbot to write in
her voice, it doesn't always cooperate. "Occasionally it writes
something, and I'm like 'Yeah, that sounds a little bit stock standard,'" she said. "So I go, 'Oh, can you rewrite it in my brand
voice again?' And it's like 'Oh, apologies. Here you go.' And that's
better, and the energy is there."

AIs' forgetfulness is just one of the reasons that we can't yet
rely on them to do our jobs for us and must review everything
they produce. The other big issue is that AIs lie constantly. This
phenomenon, which has gotten a lot of attention in the media, is
called "hallucination," though that's a bit of a misnomer. A hallucination is what happens when we perceive something that isn't
there; it's our imagination, freed from the bounds of our senses.
The word implies an altered and pathological state of mind. But

for large language models, hallucinating is simply how they operate. In order to generate any response at all, their hundreds or thousands of layers of artificial neurons have to come to a consensus on what to produce, and the process by which they do that means that the system has no ability to judge the truth or falsity of what it's spewing.

Hallucination has proved to be an ineradicable problem of all large language models, and efforts to stamp it out have been of little avail. From one generation to the next, today's AI models haven't proved to be inherently less likely to make stuff up. AI companies have reacted by feeding them ever more data on an ever wider array of topics, since they're less likely to make stuff up if they've had more training on a given topic in the first place. But as we've more or less used everything that's already available on the internet to train today's frontier AI models, that solution no longer provides any relief.

What this means is that the behavior many people default to when confronted by an apparently all-seeing oracle such as ChatGPT—ask it what it knows, and assume it's right—is a mistake. Using large language models as a source of truth can lull us into trusting their output, because they're usually right, and this can lead us to believe them when they get things wrong, which is often. One 2025 study of popular large language models found that even when AIs were asked simple, easily verifiable questions based on news articles supplied to the model, their answers included made-up information between 15 and 39 percent of the time. Another widely cited study attempted to prove, in the sense that many of us learned to prove things in geometry class, that AI hallucination is impossible to eradicate completely.

For me as a journalist, skepticism of facts, figures, and the confident pronouncements of experts has been etched into my work habits by decades of encounters with the endless ways in which people misinterpret, misremember, or deliberately misconstrue information. But double-checking everything a chatbot says can sometimes require even more time than finding the information in a trustworthy, human-generated source. Large language models fib so often and so confidently that I've learned *not* to rely on them as a source of any kind of information.

The Sixth Law of AI:
Don't trust it, and always verify its work.

This brings us back to Leanne's initial task: writing an article in about half the time it would normally take her. All the limitations outlined above go some way toward explaining why she can't just prompt an AI to write an article for her, and sixty seconds later it's done. AI, it turns out, still requires a great deal of prompting, prodding, and hand-holding plus numerous cycles of reviewing its work and asking it for revisions.

HISTORY BREAK

The Superweird Biological Intelligences
That Today's AIs Resemble Most

It's not entirely accurate to claim that today's AIs function in a way that is unheard of for biological intelligences. It's just that the creatures that today's AIs resemble aren't themselves normally thought of as intelligent.

Mycorrhizal fungi live in soil and create extensive and far-flung networks that allow them to transport nutrients and exchange them with the roots of plants. In order to build and efficiently run these networks, they exhibit a form of intelligence that has inspired scientists to describe them as "living algorithms." These fungi have no central nervous system—that is, no "brain"—yet they are capable of complex decision making about how to optimize the structure and function of their carbon-, water-, and nutrient-carrying networks.

Their cells accomplish this because they are genetically prepro-grammed with simple rules of thumb—that is, heuristics—that dic-tate how they should operate in different situations.

Other life-forms that exhibit what's known as "swarm" intelli-gence are also capable of using instinct-based rules of thumb to accomplish incredibly complex behaviors. Insects that live in colo-nies, such as ants, termites, and bees, are great examples of this.

It's entirely possible that today's AIs are, in essence, essentially gigantic, high-speed swarm intelligences. It's as if they are enormous ant colonies tasked with learning from and responding to stimuli such as human language.

As Yann LeCun, the AI pioneer who is now the chief AI scientist at Meta, once told me, "We are used to the idea that people or entities that can express themselves, or manipulate language, are smart—but that's not true. You can manipulate language and not be smart, and that's basically what LLMs are demonstrating."

There are many ways to go about using AI to write something that still leverages the knowledge, thinking, and style of an indi-vidual human being or even a whole team. The simplest is to gather up samples of your writing and attach them to a prompt to an AI chatbot in which you tell it that these are samples of your work and you'd like it to start writing in your style.

Another way to leverage AI is to ask it to help you organize your thoughts. As a writer whose continued employment depends on being better at my craft than the majority of other writers, I can't imagine using AI to write for me. But as a journalist and writer of nonfiction, the idea that an AI can act as a sort of re-search assistant and librarian is enormously appealing.

To create a first draft of an outline for the chapter you're read-ing now, I first did all the research, reading, and manual labor I would normally do when working on a book or an article. I reread transcripts of my conversations with Leanne and took notes on them. I read blog posts, scientific papers, and articles and condensed notes on those into a separate file. In all of these documents, as my brain made connections between facts and ideas, I wrote out long, meandering, and only partially coherent notes to myself, peppered with exclamation points, nested asides, and a peculiar notation I've developed over the years for flagging things I want to focus on when I'm ready to draft a piece.

My writing process, especially on really big projects, is iterative in the way of sculpture and stop-motion animation. It's as if I'm first creating an armature of ideas, layering clay or latex on top of that, refining that material, adding more layers, putting in fine details, and in the end animating my creation. It's incredibly labor intensive.

This time, instead of charging into the writing directly after throwing notes into my handful of organizing documents, I paused. I opened Claude, which, like ChatGPT, has its own form of memory, enabled by its context window. I created what in Claude is called a "project," which is a sandbox in which the AI remembers only what you feed to that particular project. Then, in a single prompt, I uploaded all of my notes, told the AI what to expect in each document I was submitting, and described in a brief prompt what I wanted it to do with them.

The specific prompt I used doesn't really matter; that's the beauty of today's large language models. While it definitely helps to communicate with them as clearly and precisely as possible, if you have reasonable communication skills, just typing at them as though they're smart human assistants is all that's required.

The outline that Claude produced from a 119-word prompt and about 2,000 words worth of notes was a little less than 500 words long and astonishingly detailed and useful. But here's the key thing: There was nothing in what it produced that wasn't already in the notes that I had fed it. Reading Claude's outline so soon after I had written the notes on which it was based, I almost felt disappointed, because it hadn't read what I had written and generated any new insights of its own.

The tendency of chatbots to at least try to do precisely what we ask—with what are often predictable and boring results—is key to their utility. In this case, Claude's ability to take documents representing what for me are disparate strands of thought, distill the commonalities, and cut out the excess verbiage is a win in terms of saving me not so much time as energy.

It's the same for Leanne, although she's willing to let the AI take the next step of writing for her. "I don't want to spend two hours writing a thought leadership piece," she said. "The topic was 'Why teams need team training for working with AI.' And I'm like 'I know this, I've already got the materials, I don't need to reinvent the wheel here. I just want to create a piece that represents me and that I'm not using up all my creative energy on.'"

In order to figure out how to incorporate AI into your personal workflow as deeply as Leanne has, there is no substitute for time and practice. Think of how everyone's phone home screen has a different array of apps on it and how that idiosyncratic mix represents hundreds, maybe thousands of hours of perfecting the workflows that person relies on their phone for.

This is one reason why Leanne describes herself as an AI "coach" rather than consultant. The overarching lesson she tries to convey, based on her own experience, is that getting over our reluctance to experiment with new AI-based tools is step one—and also steps two, three, four, and so on, as working with AI becomes a regular practice rather than a one-and-done new skill we acquire. If that sounds intimidating, don't worry; as we'll get into in the next chapter, you're *already* much more of an expert in using AI than you realize, because it's so deeply embedded in the tools so many of us use every day, whether we realize it or not.

○ TERMS

Large language model (LLM): A kind of AI trained on billions or even trillions of words' worth of content, usually scraped from public sources on the internet. LLMs are composed primarily of artificial neural networks, specifically deep neural networks, and are also a type of transformer model.

Transformer: More than meets the eye, this type of deep learning system can learn from almost any kind of sequential data. Transformers are useful for processing language, as in ChatGPT and related AI chatbots; for computer vision; for predicting the sequences of novel and useful proteins; in audio and speech processing; in diagnosing disease, and other applications.

Artificial general intelligence (AGI): In other words, human-level intelligence is the goal of many of today's AI startups. Promoting AI attainment of human-level intelligence is a good way to raise money, and a lot of people sincerely believe we're on the path to achieving it, someday. There's a huge spectrum of opinion about when we'll get there and what it will take. Given the limitations of today's AI systems, the powerful social and financial incentives pushing people to declare its imminent arrival, and the long history of people like them being wrong, very wrong, about when we'll achieve it, a good general rule is: Don't believe anyone who says it's just around the corner.

Frontier model: Also known as a foundation model, a frontier model is a cutting-edge AI from one of the many startups or big tech companies that build them. They are hugely expensive to train and equally costly to run, although these costs are rapidly diminishing due to technical innovations. Through about mid-2024, each successive frontier or foundation model was bigger than the one before it. That is, successive versions of ChatGPT literally had more parameters inside them, where parameters are the variables in a model that are tweaked when they are trained on large volumes of content. As of late 2024, this approach has led to diminishing returns, which inspired AI companies to turn to other ways to try to make their AI models smarter and more competent, but with limited success.

Machine psychology: Cognitive psychology, but for AIs.

Bag of heuristics: A hypothesis about the way modern AIs function, which remains controversial among some experts but is backed up by a growing body of research. The idea is that rather than creating an abstract, relatively compact model of the world, the way humans and other animals do, today's transformer-based AI systems learn unfathomably long lists of rules of thumb that they run all inputs through before generating output. While humans also rely on heuristics in situations where they have limited knowledge, no biological system could memorize—or reference—millions or even billions of them the way today's generative AIs, including ChatGPT, do. This means that today's AIs are truly an alien intelligence that does not function in ways that allow humans to empathize with them.

Training: AI systems, such as the large language models that power ChatGPT and its competitors, start out as gigantic masses of artificial neurons in what is usually a completely untrained, uninformed, tabula rasa state. During training, a complicated process that was first fully described in a paper by Google researchers in 2017, these transformer models "learn" the underlying structure of the data they're exposed to. (In the case of today's large language models, this is based on enormous amounts of text scraped from the internet.) Once trained, transformer AI models can be tuned, a process that adjusts the values of the variables they contain, but this tuning process is not available to end users, who must content themselves with the state of a model as it's made available to them.

Inference: When we use a transformer-based AI such as ChatGPT, our inputs are run through the tens of billions of variables inside the AI, which then spits out what it thinks is the most appropriate response. This is called *inference*. This is a statistical process—a bunch of arithmetic running on microchips, like everything else we do with computers—and should be regarded as mundane rather than mysterious.

Context window: When using an AI chatbot, the AI's context window consists of all the inputs—which can be images and even video, as well as text—that we feed to it during a work session. Because the amount of computing power required to run everything in a context window through the AI's underlying computational engine increases at roughly ten times the rate at which the data we're feeding it does, context windows are often limited in ways that can make AI chatbots seem forgetful or distractible.

Hallucination: In humans, hallucinations represent a breakdown in our sensory processing systems, but in AIs, hallucination is how we describe the process by which an AI generates new content. Thus, the process of getting real utility out of an AI is inextricable from its tendency to make stuff up. This might seem like an unsolvable problem, but there are ways to get around it, starting with limiting our expectations for what modern AIs can do.

SUMMARY

What to Know

The AI you're most likely to hear about these days is but a single small part of the giant tree of techniques and algorithms that make up modern artificial intelligence. If deep learning is a big bough jutting out from the trunk of modern AI, transformers are limbs sprouting from that bough, large language models are branches along the length of those limbs, and ChatGPT and its ilk are but twigs adorning it.

How to Think About It

Today's AIs are not intelligent in a way that we would have used that word in any age predating the advent of AI, but they are quite capable, as long as we understand their limitations and how to work with them. This includes recognizing their limited capacity to remember things, their tendency to hallucinate, and the often unpredictable situations in which they can fail.

What Questions to Ask

When using a general-purpose AI such as a chatbot, how can I customize it in order to better meet my needs? If someone claims that an AI system can operate with a degree of autonomy, ask whether humans are able to review its actions and what happens when it makes mistakes. If someone claims that their product incorporates AI, ask what kind of AI they're using and what data was used to train it. If they don't know, insist on talking to someone who does or seeing documentation that can answer your questions. If they claim that this information is proprietary, ask why you should trust their assertions about the capabilities of their system.

3

AI IS JUST SOFTWARE

You—yes, you—are almost certainly already an old hand at using AI. It doesn't matter how nontechnical or how new to experimenting with AI you are. It doesn't even matter whether you were, as of early 2025, in the half of all Americans who had never touched an AI chatbot such as ChatGPT.

If you use a smartphone and the internet and do basic tasks with one or the other, then, whether you realize it or not, you are already using AI *constantly*.

For example, I'm assuming that you google things. By the end of 2024, half of all Google searches had AI-generated summaries at the top, above the customary list of links. Just a few months later, phrasing your Google search as a question often got you something even more elaborate: a full-on dossier full of AI-generated search results broken into long bullet-point explanations, complete with in-line citations.

By the time you read this, it's almost certain that Google's "AI Mode" for search will be the dominant way that people all over the world will use search, whether or not they start at Google.com. This mode, pioneered by AI startups such as OpenAI, Anthropic, and Perplexity, dispenses with the conventional search interface altogether and instead replaces links with a clean, well-ordered list of answers, further demoting links to mere citations.

A person from April 2024, just before Google began offering AI-generated search results, who was dropped into the present day would be looking at the biggest transformation in internet search since the advent of Google itself. Someone accustomed to scanning the conventional list of ten blue links, deciding which of them to open, skimming their contents, refining their search with more googling, lather, rinse, repeat, would now be confronted by a wall of helpful and mostly accurate text requiring that they click on zero links.

Going from a world in which we search for information to one in which we're simply handed that information is a fantastic example of the Third Law of AI from chapter 1, one of the most important in this book: In the overwhelming majority of use cases, AI is a feature and not a product. For most of us most of the time, AI will be a part of other things we use, and the more seamlessly it blends itself into our existing tools and ways of doing things, the more useful it will be.

But contained within that law is the seed of a much bigger and more general idea called *scaffolding*. It's a concept that we can all apply to how we use AI while seeking out the best services that incorporate it.

Scaffolding is a broad term for the code and other systems with which developers surround AI. In other words, scaffolding is software. Imagine AI as the stones that make up an arch in a cathedral. When you build an arch, it can't stand on its own until the final stone is set into place. Until then, wooden scaffolding supports it. So, too, does today's AI depend on the scaffolding—that is, code and cloud-based systems—that surround it.

When people build AI tools for the real world, they almost always make the AI a small part of a much larger scaffolding rather than trying to do everything with some kind of AI superbrain. And because we're now more than thirty years into the age of the internet, we know that there is *a lot* of scaffolding out there already, which we can just plug AI into.

Systems built for humans—websites, apps, and the developer-facing bits of the internet infrastructure that most of us never touch directly—are also quite well suited to being operated by or interacting with AI. Google's incorporation of AI into its search engine is a great example of this. The company already has a tremendously powerful, world-straddling system for sucking up all the internet's information and deciding which bits are the most relevant to a given query. (Not incidentally, behind the scenes, that process has also, invisibly and for years, used AI.)

Adding AI to the front end of Google's search engine—the results that we see—rather than trying to replace Google's entire code base with some kind of generative AI has clearly been the right move for the company. Using AI strategically has allowed Google to remain the go-to search engine, even as many other AI-first competitors try to do the inverse and make search a mere feature of their AI chatbots.

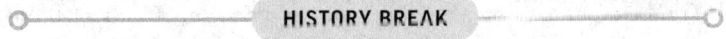

HISTORY BREAK

How Google Invented,
Then Dropped the Ball on, Modern AI

Google is a funny company. It's such a behemoth today that we almost forget that it, too, was once a scrappy startup.

Again and again, its boffins have made the fundamental breakthroughs that have enabled modern AI. But, as is often the case with giant, successful companies, Google struggles with the kind of bureaucratic issues that are an inescapable part of their size. The very thing that gives its researchers room to invent the future—seemingly unlimited resources—has at times hamstrung its ability to turn those inventions into products. (One ex-Googler who did pioneering research on AI at the company and later left described Google's paralysis as "Big company–itis. I think the bureaucracy had built to the point where I just felt like I couldn't get anything done.")

As I outlined in the previous chapter, at the heart of nearly all of the really powerful AIs that regularly make headlines is a collection of techniques and algorithms known as a transformer. It's hard to overstate the importance of the transformer in the history of AI. It's definitely a top-five all-time breakthrough. Some would rate it as the most important breakthrough in the history of the field. And it was invented at Google and revealed in a 2017 article entitled "Attention Is All You Need." The title is a reference to one of the key break-throughs in transformers, an "attention" mechanism that allows the artificial neural network at its core to come up with those endless rules of thumb that underlie modern generative AIs.

There were eight authors on that original paper. All of them quit Google not long after, either out of frustration or, like free agents in sports, to discover their true value on the open labor market. All but one of them went on to found an AI startup that was subsequently worth, on paper at least, more than a billion dollars. In 2024, Google forked over $2.7 billion to acquire a startup, a deal that insiders eventually concluded was intended primarily to rehire a single one of those researchers, Noam Shazeer. In a world full of superlatives— there are at least three AI "godfathers" and one "godmother" in the oral histories of modern AI, plus many Nobel Prize and Turing Award winners—this group's contribution is so fundamental that they're known as the "Transformer Eight."

At the time, it was clear that transformers were a cool innovation with a lot of potential, but no one had any idea how much. How could they? Imagine looking at the first steam engine, Thomas Newcomen's, in 1712. It was big, ungainly, inefficient, weak, and intended solely to lift water out of mine shafts, a task at which it was middling at best. Who could have predicted that it would lead to railroads, transatlantic shipping, the "castles of steel" that hammered one another in the bat-tle for the Atlantic in World War I, and modern steam turbines, which we still use to generate the vast majority of our electricity?

The transformer in that 2017 paper was used to translate be-tween English and German. But the researchers who authored it had an intuition that their attention-based model could be used to process all kinds of inputs, not just text but also images, audio, and video.

Their employer, Google, didn't do much with transformers at first, which was understandable, as no one yet knew their power. Some of the researchers worked in the company's translation group, so the following year transformers were incorporated into products in that area. In 2018, the company came up with the world's first transformer-based large language model, called Bidirectional Encoder Representations from Transformers, or BERT. The year after that, the company incorporated BERT into the engine that generates Google's search results.

In retrospect, adding a large language model to the inner workings of the world's most popular search engine was a huge moment in the history of AI. But at the time, it was a blink-and-you'll-miss-it nonevent. A 2019 blog post by the company's vice president of search included this thunderbolt of a line: "In fact, when it comes to ranking results, BERT will help Search better understand one in 10 searches in the U.S. in English." Yawn.

In 2021, one of the authors of the transformer paper—the researcher who was enticed to return in 2024 for $2.7 billion—left the company because Google refused to release the chatbot he'd been working on. A year later, OpenAI released ChatGPT, and so the moment when transformers burst onto our attention will forever be attributed to OpenAI and its "ChatGPT moment" and not to the company where the technology was invented.

Even so, BERT contained within itself the seeds of the current revolution in AI, powers so broad that they would lead directly to modern-day declarations by otherwise sober thinkers that AI would soon exceed human abilities.

Dustin Moskovitz, the billionaire cofounder of Facebook who subsequently founded the business software company Asana, deserves credit for introducing me to the concept of scaffolding, which is otherwise not well known outside the circles of developers who work with it. Here's how he described it in one of our conversations on the subject.

Imagine yourself setting out to perform a particular task with an AI chatbot, the way Leanne, in the previous chapter, often does—say, brainstorming a topic for an article or social media post. "First you use AI to come up with an idea, help you do research, and make an outline," said Moskovitz. "You might come up with a systematic process for doing that." So far, so good; this process is known as "prompt engineering," which is a term consultants and tech influencers use to obscure the straightforward process of "giving a chatbot instructions as you would a talented but overly literal intern."

Now imagine that you want to do this again and again. What if in the future you forget a step in your prompting, you phrase your request slightly differently, or you're using a chatbot that tends to vary more in terms of its responses? "Now you have to remember to repeat that process with the chatbot every time," said Moskovitz. "But maybe you get a little lazy about it, and then you end up with inconsistent results."

Clearly, what you need is a recipe for prompting an AI, one you can repeat with some assurance that you'll get usable results every time. It would make sense to first refine your process of talking to the chatbot through experimentation and then write it down, as a series of steps that you can follow again and again. In which case, congratulations, you've just written an algorithm, and you are now a computer programmer.

But wait, are we actually just coding when we talk to an AI chatbot? The answer is . . . sort of. The challenge here is that the responses today's large language models spit out vary from one request to the next by design. So while conventional computer programs will, barring an error, always give you the same result every time you run them, generative AI isn't guaranteed to do so.

The unpredictability of generative AI—which, like hallucination, is inherent in how these systems operate—is yet another reason that today's AIs need scaffolding. That scaffolding is built out of conventional, rules-based systems.

The overwhelming majority of the productivity gains that will accrue to humanity in the coming decades on account of AI will be achieved because of this fusion of conventional software and AI, packaged into apps and services that bear at least some resemblance to the ones we use already. Some of the most mundane examples of these new services and software are the best case studies in how this might play out because of both their simplicity and their practicality. What follows is one such example.

FREELANCER ON A MISSION

John Carrasco grew up in San Diego, a child of hardworking, entrepreneurial parents. His dad runs a landscaping company, his mother a cleaning service. After high school, John tried college and found it just wasn't for him. At twenty-one, he became a father. At the time, he was living at home, working for his dad, and doing odd jobs on the side, including driving for Uber and DoorDash.

John didn't want to live with his parents any longer or spend any more time trying to get a degree. And he definitely didn't want to keep driving for Uber while trying to care and provide for an infant. So he and his wife did the thing that so many members of Generation Z did before them: moved to a Sun Belt state where housing and jobs were more plentiful and the cost of living lower.

In Alamogordo, New Mexico, John dropped a couple of thousand dollars on some online courses to learn to do search engine optimization (SEO) for small businesses. An art as old as pre-Google search engines such as Yahoo! and Ask Jeeves, SEO remains as relevant as ever. That's because most people still start their search for a local handyman, lawyer, or service professional by typing the relevant term, plus their city or the phrase "near me," into Google.

In short order, John was picking up clients in a wide variety of industries, including service, construction, home remodeling, and even software and the law. A couple of years into building his business, ChatGPT hit the ranks of tech-savvy freelancers like a tidal wave. For someone like John, who was now working from home, juggling a dozen or more clients, and raising a toddler, anything that could make his work go faster and yield better results for his clients was a godsend. As is the case for so many freelancers and small-business owners, there was a direct relationship between his productivity and his income. He also knew that if he could cast a wider net for clients and level up to better-paying ones, he might be able to break through to a whole new level of income.

So began his quest to find the AI tools that would make him more productive—or at least the ones that would make his life easier. He has tried dozens, but almost all of them are either useless or else cost more in time and energy to use than they yield. PouncerAI was different. The way it works—and the reasons that John finds it genuinely helpful—perfectly illustrate why scaffolding is everything in AI.

The Seventh Law of AI: Scaffolding is everything.

PouncerAI is an extension for web browsers that uses AI to help freelancers apply for jobs on the biggest job board in the English-speaking world, Upwork. It does this by taking a large language model—in this case, the one that powers ChatGPT—and surrounding it with loads and loads of scaffolding so that it can perform this narrow task as quickly as possible. It can also yield results that are of far higher quality than most freelancers could manage when crafting applications for jobs on their own.

Some of what PouncerAI does, John was already doing with ChatGPT. But it was a laborious process. First, he had to copy job announcements from Upwork and paste them into the chatbot. Then he would upload his résumé and a portfolio of his work, with an additional prompt identifying all of those documents. Then he would paste in a prompt giving ChatGPT the full context of his request: He's a freelancer, he wants to respond to job postings on Upwork, here's the job, here are his qualifications and prior work, here's how he would like the prompt to sound. Then he might have to give ChatGPT additional prompts to refine its output, saying, in effect, "No, not quite like that, could you rewrite it like this?" Even after all that work, the results could be uneven.

PouncerAI reduced John's laborious—and error-prone—process to just three clicks. Now when John sees a promising job posting on Upwork, he activates the browser extension. It then runs conventional code that does everything he once did in his back-and-forth with ChatGPT, in seconds. It does this in the background, by handing all the relevant text and documents, including John's résumé, the client's request, and the custom prompts written by the creators of PouncerAI to the commercial version of ChatGPT, through an interface intended for developers known as an API.

The large language model behind ChatGPT processes that information and spits out the result, a response to the job posting. John then reviews the application in full. He often makes changes, either because of a hallucination on the part of the AI or because in his judgment something could be clearer or more compelling. (Recall the Sixth Law of AI: Don't trust it, and always verify its work.) Finally, he hits one more button to send the completed application to the person who posted the job.

It is essential that all of this happen very quickly, since people who hire on Upwork often decide on a freelancer soon after they post a job. But speed alone doesn't win the day. PouncerAI wouldn't be very useful to John if it weren't also doing a pretty good job of crafting a response to a posting that addresses the needs outlined in it by highlighting the qualifications and experience of the person applying for the job.

And here's where PouncerAI really differentiates itself: It uses language to frame job applications in ways calculated to elicit a response. Any half-decent coder could write a browser extension to do what PouncerAI does. But the secret sauce of this extension is in the plain-English prompts it uses to scaffold its requests to ChatGPT. It's like a game of Mad Libs, only the AI is being fed a mixture of documents, code, and written instructions. PouncerAI's founders understood that freelancers might be specialized in their field, but that doesn't mean they know how to craft a best-in-class response to a job ad. Even if they do, they don't have the time to do it.

"Dealing with freelancers all over the world, we found that unless you really understand things and can ask the right questions of an AI, the output is garbage," Sean Jackson, the founder of PouncerAI, told me. "Writers have frameworks; they know about things like a lead paragraph. But if I'm a programmer, I don't know what a framework is—so how will I know to ask the AI the right questions?" Freelancers, he added, "just want the answer—but with AI, the hard part is figuring out what the question is going to be."

Sean, an affable, middle-aged dad in Dallas, has a background in marketing and a special affinity for written, direct-response marketing. This is a specialty that the internet has turned into a fine art, owing to constant, quantified feedback about how well a given email or advertisement performs in terms of getting people to click through and ultimately make a purchase.

That experience has enabled Sean to create detailed prompts that PouncerAI sends to ChatGPT to push the AI model to write responses for its users in a format that will maximize responses from companies posting jobs to Upwork. These prompts are one of PouncerAI's trade secrets, developed over months of experimentation and refinement, so Sean wasn't eager to share them with me. But the internet is full of prompt libraries aimed at getting a similar result. One such prompt begins "You are a professional freelance proposal writer trained in persuasion, NLP-based mirroring techniques, and market psychology. Your job is to craft winning Upwork proposals tailored precisely to the client's job post."

Thus, part of the scaffolding of his service, which is supported by subscriptions, is his fuzzy, deeply human, hard-won knowledge of how to write marketing materials that move people to act.

For John, PouncerAI has been a game changer. Today, he is able to apply to between 7 and 10 search marketing jobs an hour, for a total of up to 160 a month. Without AI, his response rate would be a fraction of that, and even with the help of ChatGPT, all the toggling among tabs to gather all of his information into a suitable prompt would take significantly longer and wouldn't yield the same results.

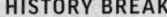

HISTORY BREAK

Will AI Kill Coding?

The answer to this question is worth trillions of dollars. Many, many companies are betting that our conversations with AIs will replace pretty much all coding. In early 2024, the chief executive officer of NVIDIA, Jensen Huang, said that kids probably shouldn't focus on learning to code, because in the future AI will take care of the messy business of writing software. By the end of that year, the chief executive officer of Google's parent company, Alphabet, said that more than a quarter of the code written at his company was being written by AI.

But as with so many new technologies, the devil is in the details. Even the most die-hard devotees of using AI to write software, using the most powerful models available, have found that using AI to code requires *constant* supervision and a deep knowledge of programming in order to keep it from going down inappropriate rabbit holes or making mistakes that could cost the companies relying on this code dearly in terms of both inefficient and vulnerable systems.

Thus, it seems that even in the area where AIs have found the greatest utility and are undergoing the most rapid evolution, we are nowhere near the point at which building software with AI is "Set it and forget it."

Notably, as with copywriting and concept art, these systems do allow a new kind of prototyping. Even nontechnical people can now use tools such as Bolt, Lovable, and Replit to use plain-English prompts to knock out working prototypes of new apps and online services. These tools don't yield systems that are robust enough to be shipped to end customers, which shows the limitations of the vogue for "vibe coding."

The simultaneous rise of code autocomplete tools that make experienced coders more productive and vibe-coding tools that can enable everyday folks to create working prototypes of software does appear to be having an impact on the demand for junior and entry-level coders. This seems less like a shift of the industry away from needing people to create and maintain products and services and more like a shift in what skills the tech industry needs those people to have.

We are moving from an era in which companies needed endless ranks of heads-down "code monkeys" to crank out lines of code toward a time when collaboration, soft skills, and imagination will be required. There is preliminary evidence that those just entering the workforce are already adjusting their goals and the kinds of jobs they're pursuing. More members of Gen Z are likely to want to start their own company on the theory that AI is creating new opportunities to do so. They are less likely to try to join a big tech company, due to the observed reality that many are laying off workers while declaring that AI is what allows them to.

There are other AI-powered tools that *fully* automate the process of responding to jobs on Upwork. These tools comb through new listings and instantly respond to the ones that meet criteria specified in advance by a job seeker. John has tried such tools and been disappointed by the results. One problem is that they apply for jobs that he isn't qualified for. Another is that the less personalized an application, the less likely it is that a company will respond to it. "The jobs are so nuanced that you really have to read the posting and have the experience to know which ones are the right ones," he noted.

The existence and shortcomings of these tools illustrate something else about AI, which we will get into in depth in the next chapter: There is such a thing as too much automation. This is something I've lived as well as reported on. For our next case study, we'll dive into my own process for getting things done.

TERMS

AI mode: Google's name for a chatbot-like, generative AI-first interface for delivering summaries of its usual searches. It's the biggest change in how humans seek information since the introduction of Google itself.

Scaffolding: All of the code, tools, and services that developers surround AI with to make it able to perform actions on our behalf. In other words, picture every webpage and app and all of the existing software that makes them possible. Now imagine adding large language models and other forms of generative AI to different parts of these existing systems. The fastest and most reliable way to build novel systems that leverage AI is to use AI only where appropriate, within existing systems. Often, that means using as little AI as possible.

Prompting: The process of giving an AI written instructions. Usually, prompts are plain-English instructions, although polyglot AIs are becoming the rule rather than the exception. Increasingly, today's AIs can also take in images, data, audio, even video as part of their prompts. Good prompting is, in many ways, indistinguishable from good programming. Both require breaking a problem down into discrete steps, being clear in one's communication, and understanding the limits of the system being prompted.

SUMMARY

What to Know

Generative AI's big bang was brought about by AI chatbots, but the future of AI is systems in which the AI is nearly invisible. The systems into which AI is incorporated can be thought of as a kind of scaffolding. Many of us are, without realizing it, already becoming experts in the use of AI, as it's been incorporated into the tools we use daily.

How to Think About It

Our innate fear of missing out or falling behind is something that those pushing their AI services and tools are naturally inclined to capitalize on. Being clear about our goals and seeking tools that serve our needs rather than bend us to their ways of operating is, as ever in technological systems, essential.

What Questions to Ask

If a tool takes over some portion of the toil of a given task, at what points are its human operators able to review and redirect its actions? What other software and services does it depend on in order to function? Is its primary utility simply that it provides access to these services, or does it allow us to use them in a truly new way that will make us more productive or improve the quality of our work?

4

AI AS PERSONAL RESEARCH
ASSISTANT AND LIBRARIAN

I have a confession to make: Despite years of researching and writing about AI, during which I talked with experts, engineers, and everyday folk about how they use it, for a long time I never thought that it would be a significant part of my own workflow. I, too, was a skeptic.

It wasn't because ChatGPT didn't seem like a useful invention. I listened to others' stories about using it to brainstorm, research unfamiliar topics, and punch up first drafts. Following their example, I tried it for myself. In the early days of ChatGPT, I used it to create a custom chatbot I dubbed "Column-Writing Intern." I told it who I was, gave it a fair amount of background on my interests and writing style, and told it that I wanted it to help me research and brainstorm topics for future articles. Mindful of its limits, I asked it to perform simple tasks such as coming up with headlines and helping me think through the outline of a piece.

But two things quickly became apparent. The first was that my job as a journalist is, basically, to do everything that ChatGPT *cannot* do—that is, obtain information that doesn't already exist somewhere on the internet and then tell stories that have never been told before. An AI trained on the *existing* text of the internet was not going to help me accomplish those goals. Even the so-called deep-research tools that came later, which have the power to scour hundreds of websites and PDFs and "reason" through the answer to a question, weren't, in my experience, any better at digging up the unique, critical nuggets of information on which my work depends.

For me, large language models seemed destined to be relegated to the most elementary tasks, for example, the autocomplete feature in Google Docs and Gmail called Smart Compose, which suggests the most likely next couple of words in a sentence, saving a fraction of a second for those willing to simply hit "tab" instead of continuing to type one letter at a time. While such features annoyed many writers, as a working journalist for whom 90 percent of my written communications are of the most mundane variety— emails, notes, transcripts—it was a nice little productivity bonus. (This feature is hardly unique to Google's products—Microsoft's version is called simply "text predictions.")

Knowing that chatbots were based on the same underlying technology as Smart Compose, it was easy for me to dismiss them as souped-up versions of what I'd already become accustomed to. I wasn't alone in my skepticism. On the internet, a derogatory name for what chatbots do cropped up. People started calling language-based generative AI "spicy autocomplete" or "autocomplete on steroids." The idea that an AI would attempt to autocomplete not merely a sentence but, based on a single prompt, a whole essay struck me as suspect. Given how often existing autocomplete features guessed wrong about what word I wanted to type next, wouldn't something that just kept going yield results that would diverge even further from what I intended?

Something else concerned me, too: a psychological phenomenon called "the anchoring effect." I knew it all too well from writing about consumer goods companies' pricing strategies. Apple loves this pricing strategy. It's the reason the company always offers an absurdly overpriced, top-of-the-line version of its phones, laptops, tablets, and watches. Consumers see that price, and by comparison, the base model device—and all the other models in between the lowest- and highest-priced ones—seems like a pretty good deal.

But anchoring isn't just about prices; it's an almost universal cognitive bias. No matter the subject, if you prime someone by suggesting a higher or lower number for something quantifiable, they will gravitate in that direction. For example, ask a group of people to estimate how old Mahatma Gandhi was when he died. Then ask another group the same question but provide a nudge such as "Wasn't he almost ninety?" Research shows that those in the latter group will make higher guesses.

Variants of the anchoring effect even show up in research on attempts to educate people about misinformation. Studies have shown that if you try to debunk a false claim, you can actually *increase* a person's likelihood of remembering the original, false claim.

If my job is to be an original thinker and AI is a tool for predicting the most likely next word in a sequence, isn't that a potential trap? The last thing I wanted to do was to have conversations with an AI that would bias me toward writing things that were just variants of whatever material from the internet the AI had been trained on. I didn't want AI to anchor my thinking to the mundane, the typical, the disposable, and the interchangeable.

But—and this was the crucial mental breakthrough for me and key, I believe, to convincing other AI holdouts—as the months went by I observed how AI continued to sneak into tools I already used. Observing that, I began to feel a little less precious about my work. I came to realize that no matter how creative your work is or how good you are at it, there is something about every job that is repetitive, tedious, draining—and best handed off to AI.

The data backs this up: By early 2025, just over two years after ChatGPT debuted, in a survey of American workers by Gallup, 45 percent said that AI has helped them become more productive.

The Eighth Law of AI:
Give it your least favorite things to do.

For me, the real breakthrough began with AI transcription. As a journalist, I am constantly interviewing people—sometimes a half dozen or more in a week, with some interviews lasting up to an hour. I had become so accustomed to transcribing interviews more or less in real time that for years I simply sat before my laptop, listening to people talk and hammering away at my keyboard. That process did no favors for my back, wrists, or disposition. At the end of a day of interviews, I felt drained, both physically and mentally.

Then a friend told me that he conducted all his meetings while pacing around his office and used an AI transcription service to convert recordings of them into text. Nowadays, you can't enter a Zoom meeting without someone's AI assistant hovering in the background, taking notes on the entire call, but at one time doing so was novel.

Thus began my exploration of a handful of AI transcription services, starting with Otter, a product that began in 2016 as a way to transcribe meetings and has evolved, like so many other AI-powered tools, into so much more.

Sam Liang, a cofounder and the CEO of Otter.ai, started the company in order to solve his own problem. "I quit Google in 2010 to build a mobile startup in Palo Alto. I had been having tons of conversations with VCs and customers and a lot of internal meetings. I found it really hard to remember all the information from those meetings. I used Google Docs to take notes, a paper notebook. But there were a lot of problems with that. I couldn't recall which notebook it was or what page it was on."

As he thought about it, what seemed like a pretty mundane issue grew into something of much greater consequence. "I realized that in the entire human history, for hundreds or thousands of years or even millions, people have been talking to each other all the time—but all that data was lost."

In 2013, Sam sold his first post-Google startup to the Chinese tech giant Alibaba and then left in 2016 to found Otter.ai. His goal: to solve the problem that had arisen for him when fundraising for and building his previous startup.

HISTORY BREAK

How Machines Were Developed That Can Understand Us Better Than People Do

Voice transcription technology dates all the way back to 1952. That year, Bell Labs' Audrey, which stood for "automatic digit recognizer," debuted. It could recognize the digits 0 through 9 when spoken aloud, but only in the voice of its creator. By the 1980s, an algorithm known as a hidden Markov model, or HMM, had made possible much more advanced voice recognition.

Then something happened that has been all too common in the development of AI: No notable breakthroughs were made for a long time. Voice recognition systems, up to and including early versions of Apple's Siri, Google Assistant, and Amazon Alexa, all used algorithms that were elaborations on the hidden Markov model. Just cramming more data into them was enough to get them to understand a wide variety of accents and voices.

As with so many other areas in AI, when transformer models came along, they blew past approaches out of the water. Researchers found that, especially with languages and accents for which there was little training data available, transformers performed much better than previous approaches had.

This is why, for so many, when OpenAI first introduced its voice interaction mode, it felt like a quantum leap forward in both comprehension and production of speech. It helped that the voice OpenAI gave its assistant was uncannily like that of the actor Scarlett Johansson, who portrayed the voice of an AI assistant that a man falls in love with in the Spike Jonze film *Her.*

Otter.ai started building its own AI models from day one, which makes it a rare bird among the current crop of AI startups, many of which simply use the frontier models made by the big players. "An important decision we made on day one was to build our own AI," said Sam. "All the transcription you see is our own in-house model—we are not using Whisper or Google AI." (Whisper is OpenAI's voice-to-text model, which was "trained on 680,000 hours of multilingual and multitask supervised data collected from the web.")

All voice transcription AIs have to cope with accents, bad microphones, and background noise. Sam, who was born and raised in China and graduated from Peking University in 1991 before coming to the United States, jokes with his team that the reason Otter's transcripts are as good as they are is that "our team needs to make sure my accent can be transcribed accurately."

Plenty of services can now transcribe meetings with some facility. Between 2017 and 2023, much of the meeting transcription done on Zoom was done by Otter. By 2024, the company had decided that the product was so central to its business that it switched entirely to its own model. Microsoft, Google, Amazon, Apple, and all of the big AI startups have their own models for converting speech to text. What was until recently a finicky technology used only by diehards willing to train systems with hours of recordings of their own voice now works right out of the box with no individualized training required and has become universal.

For me, switching to AI voice transcription was transformative because it allowed me to get creative with how I did my job. Rather than lashing myself to a desk all day, I began to treat my interviews and work calls as opportunities to get outside and go for a walk. It took months of fiddling to figure out which microphone would have the best background noise suppression when connected to my phone, so that people on the other end of the line could understand me. (It turned out that you can't beat the tiny in-line microphone on Apple's wired EarPods.)

Once I had my system down, I found I could take any kind of call while strolling through the woods near my house. They aren't just any woods; the area contains the largest wild parkland east of the Mississippi, and I was finally taking full advantage of my proximity to it. That not only eliminated the dreaded "Zoom fatigue," it also stimulated my mind and focused my attention in ways that no call made at a desk could hope to. Suddenly, I was walking miles more per day, and my dog was fitter and less stir crazy. Best of all, my mood improved.

I became an evangelist for this kind of call. I would begin meetings by telling people I was taking their call while out and about, and increasingly, people would respond with enthusiasm, saying they'd do the same. Though we were in different cities, sometimes even on different continents, I came to appreciate the way those shared walking meetings led to deeper, more engaging conversations. In time, I developed a system for jotting down the time stamp of ideas that came up in interviews that I wanted to return to later. When I got home, I would simply dump the recording into Otter. (Later, when my job mandated it, I switched to a system built for the purpose by my employer.) After a few minutes of chewing on the recording, it would spit out the transcript I needed.

Of course, not everyone needs or wants full transcripts of every meeting they attend. In early 2022, eight months before OpenAI unveiled the commercial version of ChatGPT, Otter.ai debuted a feature that provided AI-generated summaries of the meetings it transcribed.

That was the moment when my use of generative AI went from experimental to habitual. Like everyone else who is in a lot of calls or meetings, I can't always recall what they are about, much less what the key takeaways are or what I should do about what was said in them. Otter was a godsend for me in remedying that problem.

There were bumps along the way. At first, the AI-generated summaries weren't always that great. They would hallucinate things that I knew hadn't been in the calls I'd had, adding extraneous details that sounded likely enough but were just plain made up. Within a couple of years, however, the summaries weren't just good enough; they had become uncannily accurate. The system Otter.ai had created began to home in on the little but important things that struck me as less likely to jump out in an interview or meeting, even to a human reading and summarizing it.

That was my aha moment, the one everyone who spends enough time with AI has, in which they witness the system doing something that feels demonstrably on par with or even beyond the abilities of a human being doing the same job. It was unnerving—and wonderful—enough that it moved me to call up Sam to find out how his team was doing it.

Getting accurate AI outputs from sometimes meandering voice conversations is a different animal from people typing prompts into a chatbot. How did Otter.ai manage to overcome that challenge? Sam emphasized that his team had started with some of the open-source models that can be used to build chatbots but had done a great deal of posttraining and fine-tuning using the vast amounts of data Otter had already gathered. Large language models tend to be trained on written documents, which are vastly different from actual speech.

"Written documents are concise, logical, and have a certain

structure," Sam told me. "To summarize a news article is pretty easy, because if you summarize the title and first paragraph, it mostly works. Verbal communication is messy; it goes everywhere, people go back and forth, people change topics really fast, people are interrupted really often. And when you have more than three speakers, it's even more messy. It's unstructured; it flows in a different way."

Otter has continued to evolve since I first started relying on it. Its AI-generated summaries, which began as something like a brief abstract, have ballooned into an abstract plus a lengthy outline full of bullet-point highlights extracted from every part of a conversation. And those highlights link to precisely the point in a conversation from which the summarized insight derives, making it easy to scan for relevant information, then dive into the actual transcript to get specifics.

In mid-2023, Otter's capabilities took another giant leap forward: It gave users the ability to chat with the transcript of any call or meeting. Can't recall a particular fact or figure from a meeting, but you have a vague sense that someone threw one out there? Just ask the bot devoted to that particular transcript, and it will give you an answer and a link to the part of the conversation it came from. It's like having an assistant with perfect recall of everything that has ever been said in your presence.

The rapid evolution of the tools in Otter mirrors the evolution of many other language-focused AI tools. And while Otter will always hold a special place in my nerd heart on account of how it convinced me of the utility of properly applied generative AI, I now rely on a different tool chain to accomplish the same things I once used Otter for. Engineers at *The Wall Street Journal* created an AI transcription tool for our internal use, and I now dump those transcripts into Google's NotebookLM, which excels at both summarizing my interviews and answering my questions about them.

Whatever the company, the new features it's rolling out are elaborations on the core functionality of large language models. Every chatbot now offers the ability to dump whatever you like into it—documents, notes, spreadsheets, reports, video, audio—and subsequently have a conversation about the material. Even the newest, most advanced "reasoning" models are an extension of this functionality, in which large language models are having conversations *with themselves*.

These tools are getting better and better at handling things other than language, which has given rise to "multimodal" models. This is just a fancy term for models that can, in addition to language, handle images, audio, and video.

To understand how all of these advanced models work, what's likely to come next, and what limitations remain, we have to go another layer deeper in our understanding of how large language models—and their successors, multimodal models—work. To do that, we have to unpack what computer scientists mean when they say that, on a spectrum between reasoning and approximate search, what AIs are doing is more like "approximate search."

Approximate search is a combination of the rules of thumb that are encoded in the "brain" of a large language model and another very special, very fundamental element of how these models work—a kind of search algorithm known as "semantic search."

Semantic search is not merely one of the things that large language models do; it's fundamental to how they do *everything*. To understand semantic search, we have to go yet one layer deeper and appreciate how a large language model stores information.

Every word in a large language model is stored not just as a string of letters but as a vector, which is a sequence of numbers with both a magnitude and a direction. To picture this, imagine a line on a two-dimensional graph. Its magnitude is its length, and its exact orientation is its direction. Inside the memory of a computer, the values representing those characteristics are stored as a sequence of numbers. And because this vector is two-dimensional, we can represent it with just two numbers—the x and y values of the point at which it ends on a graph.

Now imagine a vector in three-dimensional space—picture, say, a toothpick in your hand. Once again, we can represent its length and orientation in space by a sequence of numbers, only this time we'll need three, for the x, y, and z dimensions.

Following so far? Well, here's where things get weird. While the human mind cannot easily visualize dimensions higher than three—that is, length, width, and height—in mathematics and computer science, there are no such constraints. Spaces of effectively infinitely many dimensions can be represented. By simply adding more numbers to the end of the list of numbers that represent a vector, it's possible to create a database of vectors of however many dimensions we like.

Creating a high-dimensional space for our vectors is important for what happens next. In this multidimensional space, we're going to plot the location of every word in a given language in relation to every other word in that language. How can we represent the relationship among the words *man, woman, child, dog,* and *cat*? If we spread them out in three-dimensional space, we're going to lose some nuances. But if we spread them out in a space of many more dimensions, we can show how one is closer to or farther away from the others with a great deal of subtlety. Every sequence of numbers associated with a given word is what's known as a "word embedding."

The reason this works is that it captures something essential about language. In 1954, the British linguist John Firth summed it up as "You shall know a word by the company it keeps." In other words, words that are close together in a multidimensional representation of them are close—or at least related—in their meaning. The more dimensions there are, the more such relationships we can represent.

But how many dimensions are required? OpenAI's GPT-3 represents every word in English with 12,288 dimensions. In other words, every word was assigned 12,288 different numbers. This allows for all kinds of subtle expressions of the relationships between words. Picture, for example, the two different word clouds you'd have to draw to show the words closely associated with the word *bank*, as in a financial institution, and *bank*, as in the bank of a river. With extra dimensions in the mix, these two very different word clouds can both be anchored on the single word *bank* but at right angles to each other—with one stretching into the fourth dimension.

How, you might ask, is the relationship between every word in the English language and every other word in the English language determined? The simplest answer is that artificial neural networks are trained on large bodies of text—say, the entirety of Wikipedia. Researchers have been doing this sort of thing since at least 2013, when researchers at Google first published on the subject. Today's large language models use vastly larger and more complex artificial neural networks and a whole host of other techniques to learn from vastly larger pools of text—at this point, basically everything available on the open web.

Here's where knowing that today's AIs represent language as an incomprehensibly large web of proximities can yield a mental model that will help us use them better: Every time we prompt an AI, we are in effect giving it an instruction that says, "Chart a unique path through your vast multidimensional vector database of words." The more elaborate and specific our prompt, the more likely we are to get an AI to go places in its vast memory where it has never gone before. This is why scaffolding, specificity, and context matter so much when we are using an AI.

The Ninth Law of AI:
Context is king.

Today's deep-research and idea-organizing AIs embody this characteristic of large language model–based AIs. To get the most out of these tools, it's essential to feed them as much of the highest-quality information and knowledge as possible.

Nowadays, if I'm researching a topic for the first time, I start by asking a deep-research tool to compile a report on it. Here's a concrete example from my own work: Not long ago, I needed to educate myself quickly about a new type of electric motor that I wanted to write about. Its underlying principle was invented centuries ago but has only recently become viable and interesting to engineers because it can be made without certain metals—known as rare earths—that China has a near monopoly on. This is an ideal use of a deep-research tool, because it is a subject about which people have written endlessly on the internet but about which I don't know the first thing.

When starting a research journey like this, I try not to overthink it. The key thing is just to begin and trust that the information the tools dig up will help me refine my prompts as I go. So, off the top of my head, I typed into the deep-research tab of Perplexity: "What is the current state of research on electrostatic motors for macro-scale applications such as HVAC systems, factories and other forms of automation? Please list any companies currently pursuing the commercialization of these motors."

Deep-research tools work by scouring the web for relevant web pages, feeding them to a large language model, and having it talk to itself about what it's learned from those pages and what it might search for next. These tools repeat the process, building up their knowledge of a subject or seeking an answer to a particular question. The result is a summary of all that the language model has extracted from the internet, with links to sources for each of its statements.

ChatGPT, Google Gemini, Perplexity, and many others are all well suited to my task. Some tools (e.g., Perplexity) tend to dive right in and quickly spit out an answer, while others (e.g., ChatGPT) have been tuned to ask clarifying questions so that they can tailor their report to my needs. If I want a quick answer, I prefer Perplexity or even just a quick Google search phrased as a question, since even Google's base search engine now attempts a kind of deep-research, AI-generated answer, and Google is continually moving more features from its "AI mode" over to its base search product. But if I have the time for the tool to think and I am eager to go deep, using a more involved tool such as ChatGPT's is the way to go.

Here's what Perplexity provided in response to my prompt: "The field of electrostatic motor technology for macro-scale applications has experienced a remarkable renaissance in recent years, primarily driven by advances in materials science and power electronics that have overcome historical limitations." Exported to a PDF, the summary alone is five pages long. It cites forty-eight different sources, including universities, industry reports, a LinkedIn post by one of the companies building the devices, articles in both mainstream and industry publications, and YouTube explainers. Perplexity generated the summary in under a minute.

I can then feed that report to a knowledge-organizing tool such as Google's NotebookLM, a project in Claude, or back into ChatGPT. These tools enable me to further summarize the report, ask questions of it, or use it as a starting point for further deep-research queries.

It often pays to use several deep-research tools in parallel. A brief AI-generated summary with inline citations on Google's base search engine is often somewhat informative, but on this occasion, the sources it cited did not line up with the assertions it made, which made them suspect. Perplexity's result was more elaborate and quickly got me to the level of understanding I needed. But ChatGPT's deep-research tool, which ran in the background as I was reading the other reports, bowled me over with the depth of its research. Ironically, perhaps, ChatGPT's output was too much for me—a mini–PhD thesis when what I really needed was a brief precis. The thing is, I didn't know what I didn't know about the topic when I started that journey, so I couldn't know in advance what amount of depth and complexity I'd need to feel as though I had some mastery of the subject. And now I have ChatGPT's report to refer to as I explore the topic further.

Again and again, I find that the results of these efforts depend far more on what I bring to the AI—my own knowledge of a subject, which can shape a prompt or allow me to feed the AI proprietary information—than on the abilities of the AI itself.

In this case, because I'd already begun talking with a company working on the technology, I knew that the applications it was targeting were more than the tiny motors in which this sort of thing had been used in the past but less demanding than the kind that go into an EV, and my prompt reflected that. I also knew that commercialization of the technology was imminent, so I made that part of my prompt as well. If I'd simply asked Perplexity the equivalent of "Tell me something about new motors," the answer would not have included that relatively obscure technology.

The ways in which I've used NotebookLM as an assistant in writing this book are instructive. Steven Johnson, the bestselling author of thirteen books, worked at Google for a couple of years to help shape the NotebookLM product. In interviews, he has said that his ultimate goal was to create a system that could serve as a repository for all of the information he needs to gather to write a book. To that end, he added, NotebookLM should never hallucinate. In my own experience, it's incredibly faithful to the documents that I dump into it—almost to a fault.

This kind of AI is what's known as "grounded" in the data that's fed into it. In a way, it uses the Gemini large language model as an advanced—that is, semantic—search engine, capable of finding what I might want in documents and taking me directly to it. While writing this book, I dumped successive chapters into a NotebookLM devoted solely to what I'd written of the book and nothing else. When I can't recall if I've discussed a topic before, I just ask NotebookLM about it, and it surfaces all the mentions of it. If I have a more complicated question about what I've said about a topic before, it can answer that, too, and quote my own writing back at me.

For all these reasons, NotebookLM has seen by far the most rapid adoption in education. Whereas many people feared that AI would be used primarily for cheating—and to be clear, it's still used extensively for that, both for writing essays and for answering questions on take-home assignments—NotebookLM shows how AI can be used to learn. A NotebookLM project isn't just a place where a knowledge worker can dump all the documents related to a project; it's also a place where a student can drop all their notes, all their reading, PDFs of research papers, and links to outside materials and ask questions of it, have NotebookLM create a podcast out of it, or make a mind map from it.

What this is all leading to is a paradigm in which AI's users are having *conversations* with documents as much as reading them. This is, of course, the most natural thing in the world; it's like asking a friend or teacher to talk to us about a subject. In the long run, as these systems get better and better at being conversation partners, it might even represent a shift back to older, Socratic methods of teaching and to an oral culture in education and away from a predominantly written one.

At its base, all of this is enabled by the vector database underpinning today's AIs. Knowing that this is what's under the hood can help us understand what computer scientists mean when they say that AIs are mostly doing an approximate search of their vast knowledge—or the documents we dumped into them—rather than producing new knowledge or truly reasoning. Even when an AI is handed fresh knowledge that wasn't part of its training data, which happens in Otter when it's parsing an interview transcript or in a deep-research tool when it's reading web pages, it's still searching across those documents, rather than reasoning with them.

This also explains why these models, which are so fundamental to today's AI revolution, have largely stopped improving and why when they're trained, they have to be so big in the first place: If they're mostly just doing an approximate search of their memories in order to generate responses to our questions and prompts, they aren't really generalizing from one area to another; they're simply charting a fresh path through their memories and organizing their responses by filtering them through an endless succession of the rules of thumb they've extracted from reading everything on the internet.

Given all that, the amazing thing about today's AIs is that they work at all. It's important to understand that they do so only because of a great deal of hand-holding and fine-tuning by both their makers and the humans that use them. They are more like search engines capable of inferring our meaning than smart assistants able to reason as a sophisticated human thinker would. They can do a pretty decent job of simulating certain kinds of intelligence. But when they work best is when we leverage their abilities to enhance our own.

With apologies to Michael Pollan, who listed rules for healthy eating in his book *In Defense of Food,* here's my personal formulation for how I use AI:

The Technologist's Dilemma
Use specific tools, not "AI."
Don't rely on them too much.
The best AI is invisible.

TERMS

Custom GPT: Many companies now allow users to create
instances of their AIs that are preloaded with instructions and
information—documents and the like—by the user. This can
be a way to jump-start the process of working with an AI
chatbot if the user knows they'll regularly want to use one
tuned this way.

Reasoning models: Large language models that talk to
themselves in order to "reason" through a problem. They are
often bedeviled by issues that arise from problems with the
large language models on which they are based; for example,
they can be brittle and hallucinate, resulting in chains of
"thought" that take reasoning models down rabbit holes that
are unhelpful or irrelevant to the problem at hand. Many
reasoning models will come up with a variety of alternate
solutions to a problem or strains of reasoning to try to avoid
these issues. Techniques from other areas of machine learning
are often incorporated into these models to train them to
come up with the correct answer to a problem—but these
approaches can have limited utility outside areas in which
there is actually one right answer, such as mathematics.

Deep-research tools: Typically, deep-research tools start with
a search query, such as a Google search, that scans the web for
documents related to a user's question. They then use a large
language model to "read" those documents and then attempt
to reason about their contents. This is why they often
incorporate a reasoning model. These tools typically conduct

multiple rounds of such research, summarization, and reasoning until they arrive (or fail to arrive) at a satisfactory answer to a user's question or have accumulated enough information to create a report that addresses it.

Smart compose or text prediction: One of the most basic and universal applications of the AIs that predate and in many respects still undergird today's large language models. Predicting the next word based on what's already been typed or spoken dates back to some of the earliest models in natural language processing, which laid the groundwork for the gigantic databases of language that make today's AIs possible.

Spicy autocomplete or autocomplete on steroids: A derogatory term for large language models that assumes they're just souped-up versions of the text prediction tools that preceded them.

Anchoring effect: A cognitive bias people run afoul of every time they make AI a part of their work.

AI aha moment: The moment you find AI has become essential to a process by virtue of its ability to match human performance on a narrow task or to speed up some step in a process.

Multimodal model: A type of large language model that can also accept and process data in audio, image, video, and other formats.

Approximate search: A combination of the rules of thumb that are encoded in the "brain" of a large language model and semantic search; fundamental to understanding both the capabilities and limitations of today's AIs. It is at the opposite end of the spectrum from what many define as reasoning abilities.

Semantic search: Searches the multidimensional space of word embeddings for related terms and concepts; fundamental to the ability of today's AIs to write fluently and to simulate reasoning.

Word embedding: The coordinates of a word in a database describing its relationship to every other word in a language, enabling semantic search and other operations useful in large language models.

Vector: In mathematics, a sequence of numbers with both a magnitude and a direction.

Multidimensional space: An abstraction that allows us to imagine a vast space in which all of our word embeddings can be stored.

Context: In large language models, all meaning is derived from the relationship of one word or concept to other words or concepts. Whereas a child learns that "apple" refers to a physical object they can touch and eat, a large language model learns only how "apple" relates to all the other words in a language. This can give us an intuition of why prompting AIs with as much information and context as possible is so important: Context is all that such a model "knows."

NotebookLM: One of a growing number of tools that can compile research done by a person or AI into a report on a subject. These reports can then be delivered in novel ways, such as through a chat interface, as mind maps, or in podcasts narrated by two AI-generated hosts.

SUMMARY

What to Know

The places in our workflows where AI might be the most useful are not often the ones we might expect. The work we find most tedious, repetitive, and annoying is a good place to start.

How to Think About It

AI's capabilities are limited by its nature, which is more of an approximate search engine for its vast database of knowledge and rules of thumb than a system that is capable of humanlike reasoning. By feeding AIs as much information—that is, context—about the task at hand as possible, we can use approximate search to accomplish tasks that would otherwise require genuine reasoning. We have to spend time with new AI tools before we can understand the trade-offs they require—usually between the quality of their work and the time they save us. When trying a new tool, there is no substitute for this lived experience.

What Questions to Ask

What novel ways of working could a new AI tool enable? In addition to making us more productive, how might those new ways of working enhance our lives?

Part II

AI FOR TEAMS

5

THE FIRST EMBERS
OF AGENTIC AI

Andrew Russo is in his late twenties and lives on the outskirts of Detroit, a city that has been through a lot of changes. In the course of several decades, it went from being the "arsenal of democracy," the broad-shouldered city on a hill that built America's vibrant middle class, to a deindustrialized wasteland that America almost gave up on during a long period of white flight and industrial decline. Now, however, the Motor City is back, part of a broader revival in America's manufacturing capacity—if not jobs in manufacturing.

At the heart of this boom in profits and productivity and the key to its jobs-lite revival is automation. The company where Andrew is head of AI embodies this trend. BACA Systems is one of countless companies that make specialized robots for manufacturing. The company's robotic systems carve the granite countertops without which no new or updated house in the United States can hope to command top dollar.

This is not a huge niche—BACA Systems' annual revenue is less than $20 million. The sophistication of the company's products and the challenges of servicing them with a small team are a sweet spot for the kind of productivity gains that can be achieved with the more sophisticated, more autonomous, but also trickier and more expensive to implement sort of AI known as "agentic AI."

If conventional generative AI is a tool for knowledge work that requires a human to wield it—in our use of it, little different from a word processor or web browser—agentic AI is the industrial robot of this kind of work. Able to operate on its own given the right guardrails and a narrow enough set of tasks, agentic AI is beginning to do to knowledge work what robotics and related automation have done to blue-collar work. That makes it vitally important for all of us to understand, whether we're a leader whose goal is to implement it in our business or a worker who will be tasked with working alongside it and must understand how it will transform our jobs.

The simplest definition of agentic AI is that it's what happens when today's generative AIs are given access to the same kinds of tools we are—everything we can access through the internet—and are tasked with using them. The canonical example is chatbot-based systems for customer service, but agentic AI is making rapid inroads into the automated handling of cybersecurity breaches and myriad systems for handling back-office tasks such as paying invoices.

The question at the heart of agentic AI is: How much agency should we grant AI? The hype around agentic AI is that it will enable companies to replace whole categories of employees. The reality is far more nuanced, and BACA Systems is a good example of how agentic AI is often used in the real world. BACA isn't replacing employees with agentic AI. The company's use of it is entirely about helping its customers get their giant, rock-chewing, industrial robot arms up and running again after a breakdown. "This is not to reduce head count," said Andrew. "We did this because what a customer cares about is the time to the first meaningful response from a service agent, and also time to case resolution."

BACA's customers are stone fabrication companies. They use BACA's robot arms—such as the Robo SawJet, of which there are more than 650 in North America—to manufacture granite countertops that are then sold to builders. BACA is primarily a software and services company that customizes standard industrial robot arms.

As with so much else in small- and medium-scale manufacturing, a work stoppage for any reason can be devastating for a stone countertop manufacturer with already thin margins. When one of BACA's robots goes down, it's a race to get it back up and running—whatever it takes.

In the past, when a customer called BACA Systems' service reps, those technicians were confronted by a mass of documents. First, there was the customer's case history: Had the robot gone down before? If so, why? Then there were the manuals for all of BACA's robots, which are continually evolving. Is this last year's model or one from a decade before? Which version of software is it running and what cutting heads? "In the past, the manual was quite literally a Word doc that's over 356 pages for one machine," said Andrew.

Before AI, sifting through all that information was the bottleneck preventing technicians from getting back to customers quickly. As we saw in part I, systems of knowledge management, such as the ones I use to write my columns, can help individuals organize masses of text and other unstructured data. But where they really shine is in their ability to collect and make accessible masses of information for teams and even whole organizations.

Andrew was the one who initiated the AI efforts at BACA. It wasn't a hard sell to his CEO, as he was already in charge of the company's knowledge management and customer support systems. Also, he didn't have to go out and buy a new system to make it work, because the customer relations management software his company was already using, Salesforce, has been very aggressive in selling its new Agentforce system to its existing customers.

When I last spoke with Salesforce CEO Marc Benioff about the company's AI offerings, he was at his house in Hawaii with two large dogs loafing in the background of our Zoom call. "With AI, it is a wow moment," he told me in the salesman patter that I'd say he has mastered, except that it seems to be his default mode of speaking at all times. "Customers that I bring it to, I say, 'Hey, look, let me build you an agent in a few minutes with your existing metadata and data and business process.' And then they say back to me, 'Oh, my gosh, we have been hypnotized into thinking that we need to build and rebuild these models and DIY our AI.'"

It's worth noting that the kind of AI Marc is talking about is now table stakes for providers of enterprise software. Executives at Asana, Box, and Microsoft have all described to me similar capabilities within their own systems, and I've spoken with customers of theirs who have made AI work on the existing troves of data they are already storing with these cloud-based companies. This is a great example of the way that AI—even agentic AI—is manifesting itself as a feature within existing software and systems, rather than as a product in itself.

Now when a customer calls BACA because its robot is on the fritz, a technician can immediately pull up an AI-generated summary of its case history. Just as important, they can chat with that case history, no matter how long it is. As a result, technicians can immediately respond to customers over email or text with, for example, "Oh, this happened in the past? You should go reset this breaker," said Andrew.

Every customer of BACA has a unique setup, full of special cases—and that insight is buried in its case history. Maybe its people have set the machine up in a highly trafficked spot where a power or data cable runs across the floor, making it prone to failure. "Maybe the breaker keeps breaking, and this is the third time, so actually maybe it's 'You need to go and inspect the cable, because there's a short,'" said Andrew. This has made it possible to resolve some customers' issues in minutes, rather than hours, he added.

What makes the AI system Andrew has built for his company "agentic" is that it's quickly evolving from a knowledge base that can leverage semantic search to a system directly accessible to customers, which allows them to help themselves. In other words, it's exactly the kind of AI-powered customer service chatbot that pretty much every company on Earth wishes it could have both to cut down on the time humans spend answering calls and to better and more quickly address customers' concerns.

To make its AI chatbot work, BACA is undergoing a top-to-bottom update of the documentation it stores for every one of the robots it has in the field. This means updating and cleaning up that documentation and breaking it into smaller chunks that can be provided to customers before they even talk with a human service rep. This system is a sharp contrast to the automation of customer service in other industries; think of the automated phone trees at businesses that we all love to hate or the AI-powered drive-throughs that are the subject of endless mockery on social media. For companies that just want to fix their manufacturing robots as quickly as possible, the ability to answer their own questions faster than any human could and in parallel with the usual service request is a competitive advantage. "Customers can log in to a portal and converse with an AI agent that knows which machines they have and all their past cases," said Andrew. "They say, 'We have this problem,' and it looks at past cases and articles and gives them an answer."

This system has started to replace many of the tasks that BACA's technicians once did when answering customer service requests, but it's not replacing the technicians. One reason is that in order to make the system work at all, those same technicians have moved from just answering calls to editing and updating the knowledge base full of articles and fixes that the company serves directly to customers.

The novel-length documents that the company's own reps used

to háve to search through when trying to help customers solve problems have been cleaned up and chunked into the smallest possible articles on individual issues and their remedies. Creating an AI system that can serve customers faster has required that the company's technicians take on a new role, but they're no less vital to the company's success—and that of its customers.

The need for BACA's technicians to invest hundreds of hours in updating the company's database is surprisingly common in companies I've talked to, and there's a simple reason for it. A well-worn principle of software engineering is the concept of "garbage in, garbage out." The first instance of this phrase dates all the way back to the 1950s. (Incredibly, a variant of it has also been attributed to Charles Babbage, who in 1821 conceived the world's first digital computer but never built it.)

"Garbage in, garbage out" applies to AI just as much as to any other software system. The most common answer I hear when I ask engineers how they reduce the rate of hallucination in their AI systems is that they make sure they feed it only the highest-quality information.

The Tenth Law of AI:
"Garbage in, garbage out" still applies.

The builders of Google's personal knowledge management software, NotebookLM, were careful to make sure that when users ask it questions that venture beyond the contents of the documents that the user has already fed to NotebookLM, it will decline to answer them. Sam Liang, the CEO of Otter.ai, told me that the number one way his company has reduced hallucination rates in its AI summaries of meetings is by making sure that transcripts are as accurate as possible in the first place. Researchers at Microsoft have shown that it's possible to create large language models that are the equal of much bigger and more resource-intensive ones simply by training their models on higher-quality data. The bottom line is that careful selection, editing, and pre-screening of the data that is fed to AIs are both essential and key to creating systems that are different and more useful than competitors'.

Marc Benioff of Salesforce is fond of saying that the opportunity for AI agents is bigger than the entire market for software—in excess of $1 trillion. And while some in AI arrive at figures just as gigantic by assuming that AI will be so powerful that it will expand the global economy by some difficult-to-believe multiplier, for Benioff, it's much simpler; that opportunity represents a significant share of the wages of the workers whose jobs AI agents will take. He calls this the market for "digital labor."

No one really knows what the market for AI agents is because it's only just getting started. Surveys of IT heads at major companies indicate that they're very hesitant to rely on agents because they don't yet trust them. This does not mean that AI agents aren't going to be used in place of thousands or even tens of thousands of workers worldwide. But early indications are that the jobs it will usurp will be the simplest, most repetitive, and easiest to automate.

HISTORY BREAK

The Biggest Breakthroughs in AI of the Past Hundred Years and What Each of Them Enabled

1936: The mathematician and World War II–era breaker of German codes Alan Turing publishes a paper that becomes the basis of modern electronic computers.

1958: Frank Rosenblatt, a Cornell University professor working for the U.S. Office of Naval Research, unveils the world's first neural network–based device, called the Mark I Perceptron.

1969: Marvin Minsky and Seymour Papert publish a book on why neural networks will never be useful for AI, causing the first "AI winter" and sending research on neural networks to the fringes of computer science for a generation.

1979: Inspired by research into the structure of the mammalian visual cortex, Kunihiko Fukushima, a researcher at NHK Broadcasting Science Research Laboratories in Tokyo, proposes the Neocognitron, the precursor of a kind of artificial neural network known as a convolutional neural network.

1998: Yann LeCun, one of the "godfathers" of modern AI, debuts LeNet, a convolutional neural network that can successfully read handwritten checks for banks.

2012: In a breakthrough year for neural networks, associates and students of Geoffrey Hinton debut AlexNet, a deep learning neural network that blows away all competitors in a contest to recognize images. Deep neural networks show breakthrough performance on speech recognition tasks and are also shown to be able to recognize cats in YouTube videos.

2016: Google's AlphaGo beats the world's best player of the board game Go, a feat that was impossible with previous brute-force approaches, such as those used by IBM's Deep Blue to defeat chess champion Garry Kasparov. Key to AlphaGo's success is the use of an algorithm known as reinforcement learning, which allows it to master the game by playing itself millions of times and learning from that experience.

2017: Researchers at Google publish the article "Attention Is All You Need," which describes the breakthrough known as transformers and gives rise to modern generative AI.

2019: Google starts using a large language model (BERT) to help process search requests.

2021: GitHub's Copilot becomes the first successful commercialization of a transformer AI, based on one built by OpenAI.

2022: The first commercial debut of a GPT, a type of large language model users can communicate with as a chatbot in the form of OpenAI's ChatGPT 3.

March 2024: Devin AI debuts; it's an "AI coder" that kicks off the craze for AI agents and agentic AI.

September 2024: The first reasoning model, OpenAI's o1, debuts.

December 2024: The first deep-research tool, Google's Gemini Deep Research, debuts.

Robert Weis, a vice president of customer service and operations at Wiley, best known for publishing textbooks and scientific journals, has been able to outsource hundreds of jobs to AI. "We used to hire agents to support our busy season, and we no longer have to do that," he told me.

For Wiley, the busy season is back-to-school time. Making sure that all the universities and bookstores that needed to stock its textbooks and other tomes could make their largest orders of the year at that time meant hiring dozens of additional temporary workers to handle their inquiries, most of which occur in online chats. Wiley had already invested heavily in a conventional rules-based software system for handling such queries—basically, a hand-coded flowchart of responses.

But as soon as ChatGPT came on the scene, Bob found that customers expected Wiley's customer service chatbot to be able to understand plain-English requests, however they were formed. They expected, in other words, to be talking with something that was on par with a human in terms of its ability to understand them. A lot of the requests were basic: People needed to reset a password or check on an order.

When Wiley switched to a large language model–powered chatbot, the rate at which it was able to close customer claims without elevating them to a human agent went up by 40 percent. "The ability to understand the customer's inquiry is much improved," said Bob.

Making the system work depended on a huge amount of scaffolding and context. Wiley already had an elaborate, well-curated knowledge base, which the company had been forced to build to power previous non-AI chatbots. That knowledge base is basically a giant FAQ full of answers to customer questions. "For our technical support, our technical escalation people generated the knowledge base, and our training people edited it," Bob said.

Bob's team at Wiley used Salesforce's AI Agent Builder to create a chatbot. While this tool can use code, it also allows people to build agents with no code at all. This ability is hardly unique to Salesforce; Microsoft, Box, Asana, and many other established enterprise software companies offer comparable tools. The result is that people who are logical thinkers and clear communicators are now building with these tools, even if they don't have any coding ability or experience. Executives at some of these companies have told me that some of the most skillful builders of AI agents are people with an English degree who have a knack for working with the Lego block–like tools that make it relatively easy to assemble AI-powered workflows in their systems.

The Eleventh Law of AI: Generative AI enables noncoders to build useful software that once required a programmer.

At the heart of this transformation in how information can be delivered to customers or used internally by companies is the way that generative AI unlocks vast troves of data that weren't usable before, what's known as unstructured data.

In the pre–generative AI era, which I spent more than a decade chronicling, the key to making systems that could really move the needle for a company was hiring data scientists to gather, organize, and clean up data. Almost all data needed to be numerical or had to be converted so that it was. Data needed to be as clean as possible, because the algorithms that were processing it—many of them just glorified statistical tools borrowed from other fields—were brittle.

But something like 90 percent of the data possessed by most companies is *unstructured* data: text, images, presentations, video, audio recordings, and the like. In other words, the vast majority of data possessed by most companies—and most individuals—is the kind that humans can generate and process. The real key to the modern AI revolution is that today's AI can take data that used to require slow, expensive humans to process and process it in the blink of an eye.

The Twelfth Law of AI:
AI makes unstructured data both accessible
and useful in unprecedented ways.

A funny thing about agentic AI is how much of it is a retread of decades-old ideas. More than twenty years ago, big companies figured out that they could automate a lot of the back-end processes through something called robotic process automation. The idea was based on the assumption that the world is full of giant companies that have invested huge amounts of money in software that requires employees to fill out forms and move data around. So why not have another piece of software do that for them directly in the software interface they were already using? Insurance companies, banks, and the like have been big users of this kind of technology.

If this sounds wildly inefficient, it's because it is. A better solution would be to simply write software that can take over all of these tasks by accessing systems and databases directly. The problem is that processes inside businesses are constantly changing and companies don't always have the resources to hire developers to do this kind of back-end coding every time something changes. Big, complicated systems are hard to change, so making software "robots" to work within existing systems—by doing exactly what a person would do, including pointing and clicking—sometimes makes sense.

Given that all this scaffolding already exists, dropping AI into software can sometimes give systems the ability to do things they couldn't before. A classic example is making mobile deposits from your phone. For reasons too numerous and byzantine to name, people still send and receive paper checks. Any system that enables recipients to deposit them by simply taking a picture of them is, by definition, using some form of AI. This brings us to my favorite example, at once quotidian and astounding, of how generative AI is transforming the way businesses operate.

Invoices, bills of lading, and purchase orders are the ubiquitous, time-tested means by which commerce gets done, without which the global economy that feeds, clothes, and shelters us could not function. Billions of these documents are exchanged every day, and a shocking number are still paper or are sent as digital documents. One estimate pegs the number of invoices businesses around the world have to deal with at 300 billion per year.

"The challenge is that each document looks different," said Petr Baudiš, a cofounder of and the chief AI architect at Rossum, a London-based company that does exactly one thing: automate document-based transactions for businesses. "You can have ten companies using QuickBooks, and each of those ten companies produces a different invoice." Before AI, that meant that every company that processed invoices in high volumes had to employ small armies of humans whose sole, exceedingly tedious job was to read those invoices and manually reenter the data in them into accounting software.

Rossum is named after the Czech author Karel Čapek's 1920 play *R. U. R.*, which gave us the word *robot*, and the company's tagline is "We want a world that builds rather than types." Solving a deeply unsexy problem well has been advantageous for the company; it was founded in 2017, has raised more than $100 million in capital funding, has more than 150 employees, and counts companies such as Siemens and Bosch among its clients, as well as the Port of Rotterdam, the most automated port in the Western Hemisphere.

Because the company is so specialized, it has broken down the processing of business documents into smaller steps, using not just transformer-based generative AI but also other vision-based AI models from an earlier era. These are still based on artificial neural networks, but they're part of the vast bestiary of AIs that were developed before transformers and that are still great at doing all kinds of tasks. (They're still powering image recognition in your phone and across social media, for example.) Processing these kinds of documents is so universal a headache and so obvious an application for modern AI that many companies have developed their own way to automate the process.

JLL, a global real estate services company, processes invoices in a way that's very different from Rossum's but still uses generative AI. For JLL, the solution has been to use an AI that is capable of operating a computer just as a human would, made by a startup called Orby AI. JLL processes millions of invoices annually, many of them manually. They can stretch to many pages and are formatted in an endless variety of ways, said Bruce Beck, JLL's chief information officer responsible for IT.

Orby works by watching people do a job on their computers—in this case, processing invoices—and automatically generates the code to create a system that can do their job for them. "We have literally thousands of people who do invoice processing," said Bruce. "I would expect us to be able to take several hundred people out of our back-office operations, because we can auto-mate this work." JLL had already outsourced those jobs to coun-tries where labor costs were far lower, so Bruce sees outsourcing the work to an AI as the next logical step.

Orby has been so good at automating invoice processing for JLL that the company is now exploring its use in handling travel and entertainment expenses and checks for fraud. Dave George, the vice president of finance technology at Amazon, has said that the company uses AI in a similar way to automate the validation and payment of invoices.

Orby was one of the earliest companies to give people the abil-ity to use multimodal AIs as complete drop-in replacements for a human sitting at a desk. But as is so often the case in AI, every other big tech company has piled into this space. OpenAI has a service called Operator, Amazon has Nova Act, Google's is called Project Mariner, and Anthropic gave its the most direct and ac-curate name possible: Computer User.

At this point, a question may be forming in your mind: If the future of AI is that we grant it ever more abilities and autonomy, doesn't that contradict the Third Law of AI—that in its ultimate form, most people will use AI most of the time as a feature of other software and services rather than as a product unto itself?

Here's why that won't be the case. As we've learned from the history of automating tasks on a computer—from scripting lan-guages to automating robotic process—these tools are wielded primarily by people whose job it is to write software and build IT systems. The reason is simple: No matter how easy you make it to program a computer, noncoders just don't have the time or inter-est. An iron law of tech adoption is that the simplest, most user-friendly way of interacting with a new technology will win the race to mass adoption every time. The future might be full of countless AI agents, but they'll be operating in the background, and when they do need us to step in and evaluate their work or steer their operations, it will be in ways that minimize the demands they make on our attention.

What's happening is the latest evolution in the acceleration of knowledge work that began decades ago. When a new technology shows up, there's a burst of excitement, but widespread adoption takes longer than many first predict. In the 1970s and 1980s, economists were baffled that the widespread uptake of information technology by U.S. businesses did not lead to increased worker productivity. Then, in the 1990s, IT finally seemed to click for businesses, and productivity grew rapidly.

In the 2000s and through the present day, productivity growth slowed again. Anyone who has had to wade into existing and often antiquated corporate IT systems—for expense reporting, payroll, digital medical records, or banking—will rapidly develop the suspicion that this second productivity slowdown is due in part to these systems' changing less over the past twenty years than we've been led to believe. The transition from doing everything on paper to doing it on PCs and the internet and mobile devices made things easier and faster but also burdened workers with the challenges of working with those systems. This is the real economic opportunity for generative and agentic AI: the low-hanging fruit at every business.

But automation isn't the be-all and end-all of this technology. In the next chapter, we'll see how it's transforming that all-too-human process that hardly anyone ever thought AI would conquer: creativity.

TERMS

Agentic AI: Pretty much any AI that has the ability to do anything beyond responding to prompts with images and text. Definitions vary widely, though, and some believe that the only true agentic AI comes from the Agentique region of France.

Knowledge base: A library of knowledge that must be updated, pruned, and tended, but thanks to AI, doesn't require the kind of structure that previous databases did.

GIGO: Garbage in, garbage out; a theme of computing and IT that recurs every time engineers come up with a new way to parse and deliver data and that becomes more important with each new generation of technology.

Digital labor: Work done by AI agents.

Unstructured data: The mess of text, images, audio, video, documents, and presentations that companies accrue and that AI excels at searching through, parsing, and surfacing insights from. The keys to this are semantic search and also the preternatural ability of today's GPTs to "remember" information across pools of data hundreds of thousands or even millions of tokens in length. Also, the opposite of structured data, which is typically the kind of quantitative data stored in traditional databases.

Robotic process automation: The automation of things people were doing on desktop computers and laptops, not by interfacing directly with the underlying systems but by creating software that interacted with other software just as a human would; a precursor of today's agentic AI.

SUMMARY
What to Know
Placing generative AI within a scaffolding of other software and giving it the ability to take actions on our behalf has led to agentic AI, or AI agents, the so-called digital laborers of our time.

How to Think About It

Using robots for knowledge work is an idea with a great deal of potential. But using AI agents successfully requires limiting the scope of what we ask them to do and monitoring their outputs, and for the foreseeable future will require humans to backstop them and take on a task when the AI agent fails.

What Questions to Ask

If a task is to be automated, what are the systems that will allow the AI and humans involved to know when the AI has gotten it wrong? What efforts will be required on the part of the humans who will use an AI agent to make it as effective as possible? In adopting AI agents, is the goal to improve the quality of work or to reduce head count?

6

AI FOR CREATIVITY

"How do you prompt AI for deliciousness?" That was the question Will Hanschell, a cofounder and the CEO of Pencil, a company that uses generative AI to create ads, asked himself and his team. The goal was simple: to create online ads for Hidden Valley Ranch, the best-selling brand of the best-selling salad dressing in the United States. But it was no small matter. Ranch dressing is big business in America, where it's the king of condiments. In 2024, Americans spent $1.3 billion on the bottled version of this buttermilk-and-herb concoction. (Bottled ranch dressing even beat bottled ketchup, which topped out at $1.26 billion in sales that year.)

Thus began a monthslong journey to create a prompt that could tell an AI image generator how to make a persuasive, mouthwatering online banner ad including the Hidden Valley brand identity, its colors, and the company's particular style of photography. At the same time, the prompt had to push the food in that ad out of the uncanny valley of plausibly edible and up to the heights of photorealistically scrumptious.

Some people's dream is to create a perfect recipe for ranch dressing. For Will and his team, their dream was creating the perfect recipe for prompting an AI image generator to create exceptionally appealing images of the foods to go with that dressing.

They would use OpenAI's Dall-E for the ads that required more creativity and Google's Imagen for the ones that needed to look more realistic. Here was the prompt they started with:

> Generate a minimalistic top down photographic flat lay view with a background that's yellow, background is a solid color, chicken wings on a plate, there is a striped cloth to the side, plate of fries and Ranch in a small saucer. In the style of 32k uhd, natural lighting, well lit, authentic, real, clean, modern looking, crisp, sharp and clear image, photorealistic, studio photography quality.

But the early results weren't good enough. Pencil had been given the ranch dressing challenge by Nicole Thomas, the director of marketing transformation at Hidden Valley's parent company, Clorox. Thomas had hired Pencil because she wanted to upend how her entire company makes ads. Usually, this process is a slog of paying a food stylist and photographer to take suitable photographs, then assembling them into ads in Photoshop. With AI, she thought, it should be possible to create such images in an instant with nothing more than a prompt from a graphic designer. And so she was prodding Pencil to up the ante. "Will, we need it to be more delicious—we need it to *look* more delicious," she told him as she looked over one particularly tricky ad, which paired a bottle of the dressing with a plate of spicy wings.

Will turned to a colleague. "And I'm like 'Oh, my God, how do you explain to AI what deliciousness is?'" He fretted, "I'm asking myself, 'Is it about how moist the wings are? Is it the color? Is it about how crispy?'"

Getting to the next level of realism and appeal for those images required instructing an AI chatbot to create a "prompt improver," which could refine the sequence of text that was subsequently fed to the image generator. In other words, the team started by first asking a chatbot how to write a better prompt for an image generation AI. Experienced prompt engineers know this trick, by which they ladder up to an ideal prompt by going back and forth with a chatbot in a conversation about how to write the best possible prompt to achieve a specific goal. It's an especially potent trick to use when creating prompts for image generation AIs, since they aren't language based in the same way that chatbots are and work best when prompts are tailored to them beforehand.

This was the end result, a prompt in which everything in brackets could be swapped out to create whatever ad type was required:

A bright and appetizing flat lay shot featuring a [main dish] sliced/arranged neatly on a [plate type] plate. The dish is styled with [garnishes] and paired with a small bowl of [side sauce or dip] on the side. Set on a [background color] surface with a [type and color of textile, e.g. striped or linen] kitchen towel casually draped in the scene. A realistic [product or packaging] is placed in the foreground, partially overlapping the plate for a bold, product-forward composition. Lighting is clean and diffused, with soft shadows enhancing texture and freshness. The overall tone is [mood: e.g. cheerful, fresh, inviting], ideal for a food advertisement or brand showcase.

The result, when the team customized the prompt for chicken wings, was a conventional, square banner ad featuring wings that look completely photorealistic sitting on a shiny green plate on which even the shadows and reflections are true to life, paired with a bottle of Hidden Valley Ranch dressing. The first time I saw it in a lineup of similar images, I asked which were AI-generated. "All of them" was the response.

When Nicole saw the ad and many others like it, featuring a variety of foods, she knew that not only did she have a winner for that ad campaign but the team at Pencil had created a system for AI-generating ads that was robust and could be used again and again.

Clorox is in the midst of a five-year, $500 million investment in its internal IT infrastructure—one of those "digital transformations" that every company on the planet is perennially committing to—and much of it is about infusing AI into almost everything the company does. When companies claim nowadays that AI is at the center of a tech overhaul, my eyebrow goes up. AI is now ubiquitous in software and IT systems, from sales to cybersecurity. The unavoidability of AI means that for most companies, saying your business uses it is like boasting that it gives its employees laptops. Clorox's success in incorporating AI is mostly about how grassroots it's been. Across the company, teams I spoke with had arrived at different varieties of AI on their own.

The company's success in making AI work for its advertising is based on the fact that image generators have been rapidly improving. In 2023, a video generated by an image generator, of the actor Will Smith eating spaghetti, went viral because it was so bizarre and horrific. But by the time the Clorox and Pencil teams were using the technology in early 2024, generating photorealistic images was a solved problem. As I talked with them, they showed me page after page of ads they'd generated with AI—of people filling Glad trash bags, of a half-dozen different snack foods being paired with ranch dressing.

At one point I asked for clarification about which elements of the ads had been generated with AI. Oh, they responded, *all of them*. Everything in the ads? Yes, the ads had all been completely generated with AI.

That was the moment I realized that none of us, no matter how savvy we think we are about detecting the telltale signs of AI-generated content, can trust any image or video we see on the internet ever again.

The Thirteenth Law of AI:
AI can create photorealistic images, video, and
audio so convincing that they are rapidly infiltrating
the media we consume—without our knowing it.

Part of what's going on is that what were until recently relatively primitive image generation systems—prone to all sorts of errors from mangled text to polydactyl hands—have been fused with transformer-based large language models. The result is what's known as "multimodal image generation." In the simplest terms, it means that image generation systems can now be directed in ways that are as sophisticated as the ways in which we prompt conventional large language models.

So, for example, it's now possible to tell both Google's and OpenAI's models (and, by the time you read this, pretty much everyone else's) to generate an image and get a faithful rendering of what you asked for in whatever style you like—from an uncannily faithful interpretation in the style of Studio Ghibli to photorealistic. In a way that can be intoxicating to play with, these models can handle obscure, creative, and truly outré requests.

For example, in order to test the abilities of these models, I dropped this prompt, which I made up off the top of my head, into Google's 2.0 Flash (Image Generation) model:

> I'd like to put your new multimodal image generation abilities to the test. Please generate a poster for a fictional liqueur, called "Feu à volonté" in a style typical of the advertising posters of the Art Nouveau era.

The results aren't anywhere close to suitable for final use in an ad campaign; they are, at best, concept art. The image is fuzzy, and the extra text on the poster is still the usual image generation model gibberish. But the fact that the model mostly nailed it in other respects shows how far these systems have come in just a few short years.

Tasking the image generator with the kind of direction you might give a human designer is instructive, as you almost immediately run up against further limitations of the system. I followed up with this prompt:

> This is great, but I'd love for you to do something with the image that plays with the name of the liqueur. "Feu à volonté" is an idiomatic phrase that literally means "fire at will" and is the equivalent of "bombs away" in English. Could you recreate this image but take it in a direction that plays with the underlying meaning of that phrase, while keeping other characteristics of my previous prompt?

The image generator responded with a poster in which all of the text is mangled. And it's failed to understand the idiomatic phrase, even though I had emphasized and explained it, leading to an overly literal interpretation of my prompt that doesn't play with its underlying meaning. In a failure typical of image generators, which can't parse language in the way that large language models can, the system homed in on just one word: fire.

As ever, a little experimentation with an AI model quickly reveals what it's bad at. Discovering what it's good at takes much more work.

It helps to try different systems. Google generated those images very quickly—in seconds. Putting the same request to OpenAI's GPT-4o, which also has multimodal image generation abilities, meant waiting for minutes for a result. As of this writing, this isn't atypical, since image generation is far more computationally demanding than simply bantering with a large language model and is on a par with putting a question to the most involved deep reasoning models. Every single one of these systems follows a law

I call Huang's Law. We'll explore it in detail later, but briefly, Huang's Law, like Moore's Law before it, describes the ways in which computers are becoming exponentially faster at performing AI tasks for us.

Is the image ChatGPT generated better? It's definitely clearer and more direct, but it feels more like a cartoon reinterpretation of the style of an era than a faithful reproduction of it. And no human designer would ever make the mistake of putting the word "Liqueur" on the poster twice—it appears at both the top and bottom of the image.

In some ways, this is an unfair test of the abilities of these models. They are, fundamentally, unsuited to handling words and language and far better at generating images without them.

Then I tried Clorox's approach: Generate an image only and worry about fixing the text afterward in Photoshop. I dropped Clorox's actual prompt into Google's image generator, with my own preferences included:

> Please generate a photo-realistic image of a bright and appetizing flat lay shot featuring chicken tenders neatly on a ceramic plate. The dish is styled with lettuce and paired with a small bowl of ranch dressing on the side. Set on a green surface with a linen kitchen towel casually draped in the scene. A realistic Hidden Valley Ranch dressing bottle is placed in the foreground, partially overlapping the plate for a bold, product-forward composition. Lighting is clean and diffused, with soft shadows enhancing texture and freshness. The overall tone is festive and inviting, ideal for a food advertisement or brand showcase.

The result was an image eerily similar to what Clorox's team regularly generates with its own AI. The ranch dressing bottle is far from perfect, but it's easy to see how a single designer, equipped with these tools, could fix that afterward and produce an endless array of suitable product shots without ever having to go to the trouble of working with a photographer or food stylist.

The results of almost exactly the same prompt in the image generator accessible from GPT-4o yield similar results, only this time, the AI almost nailed the Hidden Valley Ranch bottle: the shape, the speckled off-white of the dressing itself, and for the most part the logo. But, hilariously, when I look closely, I notice that this is in fact an off-brand bottle of "Hidden Yalley" Ranch.

Also, bizarrely, there is a ghostly silhouette of a Mercedes-Benz sedan in the background. And then there's the too-perfect way in which the sliced chicken has been arrayed on a piece of lettuce, which seems to have been genetically engineered not to have a stem.

○———————————— HISTORY BREAK ————————————○

Where Did Image Generation Models Come From?

At least some of the hype around AI came about because AI image generation arrived about the same time as ChatGPT. The temporal coincidence of human-sounding chatbots that appeared to think and image generation models that seemed able to illustrate any stray thought we might have was a low-key sensory assault that made AI, as a whole, seem like something magical that was arriving all at once.

But the simultaneous arrival of those two distinct types of AI was just that: a coincidence. Both were made possible by the same en-abling technologies: artificial neural networks, deep learning, cheap and widely available computing power courtesy of data centers full of (mostly) NVIDIA GPUs. But the first public image generation models actually predated the arrival of ChatGPT and were based on a distinct technology.

The underlying algorithm is known as diffusion. The highest-level explanation of how it works goes something like this: Imagine taking an image; it could be anything, but let's say it's a web comic–style one of a cat riding a unicorn. Now add some random noise to this image, the sort that would show up as grain in an old photo-graph taken with film in low light. Ask a neural network to remove the noise and restore the original image. Do this over and over again, adding in more and more noise. Eventually, you'll get a deep learning system that can be given an image that consists *only* of random noise, which can then "denoise" it all the way back to the original image.

This sounds crazy, I know, but the history of AI is full of research-ers more or less stumbling about on a random walk, testing and dis-carding hypotheses about new algorithms, borrowing liberally from everything from particle physics to the architecture of the human brain. Most experiments don't work out, but occasionally something advances the state of the art, and the whole research community piles on. Periods of relative stasis are followed by rapid advance-ments. This is basically the history of image generation systems over the past decade.

What makes today's image generation models so capable is that they aren't just trained to generate a single image, our unicorn-riding cat; they're trained on vast arrays of images, generally scraped from all over the internet. (The ethics and legality of using all that human-produced material without paying its creators are subjects of ongo-ing debate and litigation.) By attaching a large language model to an image generator, today's models are able to translate plain-language prompts into images.

But the process is far from perfect, because these are still two distinct kinds of AI: a transformer-based large language model and a diffusion-based image generation one. This is part of the reason that early image generators could yield such uneven results and why generating prompts for them was an art. It's also the reason why these systems remain imperfect in their ability to follow instructions and limited in their ability to simulate human creativity.

So what led Nicole from Clorox to get in touch with the team at Pencil to help with the Hidden Valley Ranch campaign?

Founded in 1913, Clorox is a century-old company still head-quartered in beautiful downtown Oakland, California. Despite being a household name, it has net sales of less than $8 billion a year, making it a relatively small fish in a country full of consolidated giants. In 2024, it just barely hung on to one of the bottommost rungs in the Fortune 500 list.

Its relatively modest size—eight thousand employees worldwide—and proximity to Silicon Valley are reasons that the company has been unusually quick to adopt AI. In a world in which corporate leaders are typically either tech companies or startups, Clorox is that rare bird, a company with enough re-sources to invest in overhauling its processes with new technology but not so big or hidebound by tradition that it's unable to move quickly to incorporate what works.

"We've been burned over the years by tech companies over-promising," said Nicole. Clorox's senior vice president and chief R&D officer, Michael Ott, said that in his department, he'd had to screen more than a hundred different companies and their AI products before settling on just six that actually worked for the company.

As I came to understand the range of AI tools everyone within the company used—from innovation and customer research to supply chain management, marketing, and advertising—I was impressed that some had come from small startups such as Pen-cil, while others were from giant tech companies, such as Adobe. There was no hard-and-fast rule for the size or tenure of the companies that made tools that actually worked, people in every division said; the criterion was just whether or not the tools ac-tually did.

"It took experimentation, trial and error, learning what works, and then scaling what works right," said Will, reflecting on what his company had learned from the peculiarities of AI-generated ads that include food. "Once you've learned how to describe chicken wings in a delicious way, then you can talk about burritos in a delicious way. So there's some up-front learning about how to prompt the model and then scaling that across everything else." Even the taglines in the company's ads—puns such as "Unburrito-ble flavor!" and, in an ad featuring a TV remote, "Plot twists and tater tots!" were written by AI.

I've talked to a lot of creative people about AI. In Hollywood alone, I've spoken with everyone from anonymous concept artists who help define the look and feel of a movie at its earliest stages to the Russo brothers, who directed the second-highest-grossing movie in history, *Avengers: Endgame.* The attitude is always, understandably, that AI ruins creativity because it's cheating.

But in advertising, I have found that no one cares. Few in that game have any illusions about their line of work—long gone are the days of Mad Men and the mythos of Madison Avenue. In the age of algorithms, the endless scroll, and targeted advertising, all anyone in the industry really cares about is whether or not ads work.

This doesn't mean that AI is a magic bullet, when it comes to advertising, marketing, and promotional material. "People think that 'Oh, because AI made an ad, it's magically going to perform better,'" said Will. But that's not the case. What makes AI useful for creative teams is that in the time they could previously have produced a couple of ads using conventional tools—stock or in-house photography, Photoshop, humans brainstorming—they can now make ten.

For ranch dressing specifically, this is a game changer. Executives at Clorox have declared it their mission to get Americans eating *a lot* more of the stuff. "We want there to be ranch occasions at every hour of the day," one executive has said. "Breakfast is one of our new ways in."

This means creating rafts of new ads pairing the hyperpalatable dip with every snack food you can imagine, from pizza and nachos to pretzels and gyoza. "Because you're making it more relevant, more personalized, more tailored to what snack someone likes, that also has a bearing on performance," said Will.

For Nicole, this means creating a boatload more ads to throw into the voracious maw of the ad-targeting engines dominated by Meta, Google, and Amazon. "We can create a template to then prompt gen AI to populate relevant images and messages or positions or calls to action," she said. "So effectively, within minutes, we can have hundreds of personalized creatives to then serve to different audiences."

It's not hard to see how that personalization is of a piece with the personalization afforded by an AI research assistant with a long-term memory, such as ChatGPT, Gemini, Claude, or NotebookLM. AI is, in the broadest terms, a way to leverage the vast amounts of data we throw off to change our experience of work and the world—in ways both good and bad.

The Fourteenth Law of AI: Generative AI enables previously unprecedented levels of personalization.

Where generative AI can feel as though it's sucking the life out of the creative professions, such as writing novels and drawing comics, advertising feels like the perfect application for it. Clorox is now using it for more than 80 percent of the imagery and copy for online advertising and product landing pages the company produces. It's led to an increase in the performance of some ads— 10 percent better for ads for Glad trash bags, said Nicole—which may sound modest but is big in a world in which every percentage point counts.

"VIRTUAL" PRODUCTION AND GENERATIVE FILL

There's one other area in which the advertising and marketing teams at Clorox have found AI especially useful: combining real-world imagery with AI-generated settings.

This is a great example of how limiting the scope of what we ask of AI and combining its output with conventional techniques can yield the best possible results, while reducing the amount of time and resources it takes to create a piece of content.

Many image-editing programs now have the ability to use AI image generators to swiftly create alternative backgrounds for existing photos. Clorox has tested this with its Kingsford charcoal brand. In a way, this is a kind of green-screening process: Photographers do a conventional shoot of someone grilling with Kingsford and then use a tool such as Photoshop's Generative Fill to swap out the background. Need ads that can pitch grilling as something you can do by the pool in the summer, in the woods in the fall, and in the backyard in the spring? It's as simple as swapping out the background with an AI-generated one.

One challenge with this kind of approach is that it can look less than completely natural—generative fill on an image after it's already been shot is never perfect, and making it work for video generally requires a green screen. As a result, many photographers and videographers are turning to a technology that was, until recently, the domain of big Hollywood studios: virtual production.

In virtual production, instead of using an image editor to replace the background of a shot, photographers and videographers put a subject in front of a wall-size array of bright, high-resolution, high-contrast flat-panel displays. The most elaborate of these setups can surround a subject on four sides—left, right, back, and above—with displays so bright that they are the primary lighting sources, leading to realistic lighting and reflection effects.

Virtual production is especially popular for shooting that staple of TV and movies: two people talking while driving in a car.

Its most famous early-use case was the *Mandalorian* series on Disney+, in which it allowed directors and producers to immerse characters in rich outdoor science fiction settings, such as a desert planet with more than one sun, without actually having to move the actors and crew to a desert.

The team at Clorox uses just one virtual background, a large wall that can be placed behind subjects using products. As with generative fill, these backgrounds are generated by AI, said Nicole. The technology is especially well suited to this kind of work because, of course, the point of a background is for it not to be the focus of attention; it might even be out of focus.

In the next chapter, we'll stick with Clorox as a case study in adopting AI across the organization. But we'll be going in a very different direction, on a journey across the huge landscape of types of AI that defined the field for decades and that are still essential for data-driven businesses ranging from manufacturers to insurers.

TERMS

Image generator: A diffusion-based AI that is trained by steadily adding noise to images and having the AI learn how to remove it to restore an image. After training on a broad enough array of images, such an AI can eventually start with a picture that consists solely of random noise and denoise that into a user-specified image. (Technically speaking, the noise is Gaussian.)

Multimodal image generation: A closer fusion of image generators with large language models has made the former more responsive when prompted through the latter. This has made it easier to revise images, feed them sketches as a starting point, and give them specific directions about what we want. The result has been image generators that are much closer to an ideal state in which they can be prompted to generate near-final imagery, but there remain many flaws in this approach on account of these two kinds of AIs working in fundamentally different ways.

Ranch occasions: Clorox corporate speak for the company's attempt to convince Americans that any time of day is a good day for ranch dressing. (It's working.)

Generative fill: Traditional image-editing tools and AI-first image generators have both gained the ability to replace user-defined parts of an image with AI-generated content. Making it easy to fuse real images with AI-generated ones enables new kinds of flexibility for art directors while preserving the parts of an illustrator's or photographer's art that is most important for creating something distinctive and grabby.

Virtual production: As an alternative to green screen and generative fill, photographers and videographers are leveraging a profusion of new systems that replace the walls of a studio with arrays of flat-panel displays seamlessly joined at the edges. These displays can show AI-generated imagery in something that approximates a real-life version of the holodeck from *Star Trek*.

SUMMARY
What to Know
Image generation is an area in which AI is improving quickly on account of better scaffolding to link large language models and image generators. While its output is generally good enough only for concept art—an area in which its use is controversial—it's already good enough to be used for advertising. The combination of AI-generated imagery with traditional illustrations and photographs may prove to

be the sweet spot for this technology, just as the fusion of a skilled writer with an AI research assistant and thought partner can work best in that field.

How to Think About It

Image generation is a technology distinct from what we've learned so far about the underpinnings of large language models. In addition to its impact on illustrators, photographers, and videographers, its rapid advance means that we can no longer trust any image or video we see on the internet.

What Questions to Ask

When determining what role AI-generated imagery can play in a business, it's important to start by asking about the importance of authenticity and sincerity in relation to your audience. In using AI-generated imagery, how do we balance the desire for better performance of a piece of content, either on social media or in targeted advertising, against the risk of seeming inauthentic?

7

"CLASSIC" AI

Eric Schwartz is an energetic fiftysomething with colorful eyeglass frames that match his youthful energy. His enthusiasm for his work at Clorox makes it sound way more fun than his title—senior vice president and chief marketing officer—might suggest. It helps that, unlike pretty much every other chief marketing officer I've encountered, his role goes way beyond taking interviews and being in charge of marketing.

In the previous chapter, I talked about how Clorox is using generative AI in advertising and marketing. In this one, I'll talk about the many other, older kinds of AI companies use and why they remain so vital.

One of the challenges of talking about AI is that people have very different definitions of it, depending on their history with it. For people whose first direct encounter with AI is ChatGPT, AI equals generative AI. This is a problem, because generative AI, as big as it has become and as rapidly as it's evolving, is actually a tiny speck in the vast ocean of techniques that qualify as AI.

A useful analogy for describing the evolution of AI is evolution. In this framing, the latest version of ChatGPT is an apex predator—a swift, clever, market-devouring velociraptor. But that doesn't mean there aren't countless other life-forms in the vast ecosystem of artificial intelligences, all of them evolving at their own pace. They might not be as exciting as ChatGPT or as sophisticated; they might be the AI equivalent of algae. But—at the risk of straining this ecological metaphor—algae and bacteria are what actually matter in terms of the maintenance of a habitable biosphere. So, too, in the hierarchy of AIs on which humans depend are the less exciting, less complicated, older kinds of AI that matter most.

Unfortunately, the rise of generative AI has captured most of our attention and made it difficult to talk about any other variety. Partly this is because generative AI is flashy. It's easy to demo—and thus it appears to be vastly more capable than other flavors of AI in a way that suggests it might usurp all their roles. But this is not the case. It's like saying that every ant needs the brainpower of a human being because humans' brains are so much bigger and more sophisticated than an ant's. Can you imagine what kind of a world we'd live in if every ant had to drag around a three-pound human brain? Aside from the fact that the energetics would never work out, it would be really unsettling, all those brains lying about with useless tiny ant bodies attached.

Fortunately, evolution doesn't work like that, and technocapitalist industrial systems, which are governed by similar rules, don't, either. Businesses tend to use the AI they need, where they need it, and every incentive, from its cost to its complexity, pushes them to use the right amount of AI at the right time in the right places.

The Fifteenth Law of AI:
"Classic" AI is far more important for the operation of our world than generative AI.

This is why what is arguably Clorox's most important AI system is not generative AI; it runs the company's integrated business planning, or IBP, system.

IBP systems are common in the consumer packaged goods industry and are also used by a broad range of retailers and manufacturers, large and small. At its most basic, IBP is the process by which a company decides how much of what to make, where, and when. This is an unusually tricky process that can be costly to get wrong in terms of either not making enough to meet demand or making too much and ending up with a bunch of extra inventory on hand.

Because so many other parts of the business affect the question of how much to make of a product, integrated business planning means having to pull in data from sales and marketing, since advertising a product can increase demand; finance, because you have to decide how to spend the company's money; supply chain planning, because you have to decide how much to make of a thing and how to distribute it; and the rest of operations, because every other moving part of the company can also have some influence. "The core integrated business planning instance for Clorox is absolutely not generative AI; it's predictive AI, and it's using machine learning techniques," said Eric.

If we spread the taxonomy of AI across a timeline of the history of computing, almost the entire history of AI is about the creation of everything *but* generative AI. Nearly the whole timeline is full of variants and elaborations of the other type of AI: *discriminative* AI.

Discriminative AI is what almost everyone was talking about pretty much right up until the moment that ChatGPT and image generators burst onto the scene in 2022. (AI researchers were working on generative AI well before that, but few outside their specialty knew about it.) It is the type of AI used in image recognition, for example, in the systems that can identify faces in your photographs. It's also used in sentiment analysis, as in what marketers use to determine if people are saying good or bad things about a brand, product, or politician on the internet. It's used in fraud detection, such as the kind that automatically rejects suspect charges on your credit card. It's also used in medical diagnosis, spam filtering, and the list goes on. Related, some might say interchangeable, terms for discriminative AI are "predictive analytics" and "predictive AI."

Not surprisingly, predictive AI is used to predict things. And in Clorox's IBP system, predictive analytics are used to predict how much of a given product the company should make and to which retailers it should be distributed.

Take one of the products most closely identified with the company, Clorox disinfectant wipes. For most of the history of IBP, the primary indicator for the company when it came to how many wipes to manufacture was data about how many of them people had bought in the past. If the numbers say that people buy more during cold winter months, when they're more worried about catching colds and the flu, you probably want to manufacture more of them a few months in advance so they can arrive on store shelves in time. Any updates to such predictions were hashed out in meetings in which sales reps would hazard their best guesses about how much a company such as Walmart might be modifying its traditional seasonal order.

That kind of manufacturing and inventory planning relied on statistics. Roughly speaking, if you could draw a curve on a sheet of graph paper that reflected variations in demand over a year and tweak it with a few other inputs, such as what retailers had ordered in the past few months, that was your prediction of future demand.

But AI—that is, classical predictive AI—provides a much more flexible and accurate way to figure out how much of a thing to manufacture. The same mathematics that make possible targeted advertising, traffic prediction in a mapping app, and automated evaluation of medical scans now underpin Clorox's systems for predicting demand.

The company's AI-based IBP system is rooted in machine learning, which these days is often (yet another) shorthand for nongenerative—that is, discriminative—AI. Machine learning systems can be based on all kinds of underlying algorithms and mathematics. But for the most part, companies are going with deep learning systems. Deep learning is also a part of large language models, chatbots, image generators, autonomous driving systems, and the like, but all of which go far beyond traditional machine learning systems in ways that make them generative, rather than discriminative AI.

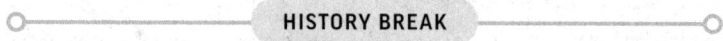

HISTORY BREAK

How Statistics Became AI

One of the jokes about AI until recently was that it's just statistics. This isn't quite fair to either AI or statistics. And as systems become vastly more complicated, it's becoming less and less the case.

But there is a grain of truth in the joke. Before there were neural networks or even earlier systems, such as Boltzmann machines and Markov chains, there was regression. If you've ever spied a chart in a scientific or economics paper in which a spray of dots across a graph is bisected by a line and the line represents the relationship between two things, that's a kind of regression.

The question is simple: What's the relationship between two things? For example, what's the relationship between outside temperature and crime? This, it turns out, is a fairly straightforward one: Above a certain temperature, the hotter it gets, the more crime there is in the average American city.

But how do we know this is true—that is, how can we *prove* that it's true? Being good social scientists, we gather as much data as we can. In this case, it's all fairly accessible: crime rates in major American cities on a daily basis, the temperature on each day. Then we plot the data on a chart. Now we use regression to find the line that best fits the trend. For some things, it might be a straight line, but for this particular case of temperature versus crime, it's not. Above 85° F., crime goes up much faster with each increase in temperature than it does below that. Complexities mount, and a straight line won't adequately describe the relationship between the two variables. We need a more complicated equation to describe the curve that best fits this data.

With this most basic building block—the best curve to fit an observed pattern of data—incalculable numbers of machine learning systems have been built. Even the most sophisticated AIs, the transformer-based ones at the heart of today's frontier models, are conducting a kind of regression analysis. When data scientists and AI engineers talk about their systems "overfitting" to a set of data, leading to a model that can't cope with the real world, what they are referencing is a concept from statistics, one that predates modern computing. What they mean is that their model has learned a given data set too well and can now make predictions that are valid for only that particular pool of information.

The mathematics that underlie today's AIs, mostly calculus and linear algebra, is of course quite old. In chapter 5 I mentioned Frank Rosenblatt's Perceptron of 1958, the earliest device resembling a modern artificial neural network. Unlike today's deep neural networks, which have many layers of artificial neurons, his Perceptron was "shallow" because it had only one layer. In its operation, it was mathematically identical to a simple regression model. What made it a "learning" system was that it could be trained to discover the function that yielded the correct result. It "learned" rather than being programmed. Thus, modern neural network–based AI was born of a device that was just, at base, figuring out elementary statistical relationships—but importantly, *on its own.*

The alchemy that made the Perceptron possible was the computer. The initial version of the Perceptron was implemented in software and required punch cards for programming and a powerful IBM mainframe. A later version, the Mark I, made with custom electronics, could operate much faster. Incredibly, it still exists; the original Mark I Perceptron is now in the Smithsonian Institution.

The transition of the Perceptron from unusably slow when implemented on one of the most powerful computers of the day to usable when reimplemented on custom, dedicated hardware, would play out again and again during the history of AI, up to the present day.

When pioneers in the field of AI, such as Yann LeCun and Geoffrey Hinton, first built their neural networks, the main reason they couldn't do much with them was that the hardware of the day wasn't fast enough to make them usable. That also limited the amount of data the systems could ingest—that is, be trained on. Researchers would later discover that amounts of data far greater than they had guessed were required to make these systems capable of doing the things that early neural networks soon proved to be best at, such as recognizing images and translating speech into text.

The line from statistics to today's deep learning systems is not a straight one. The path was winding, with many dead ends and insights borrowed from neuroscience, statistical physics, and other disciplines. But a key feature of today's systems remains, at their core, the way they transform the data they ingest into an abstraction that captures the statistical distribution of that data. In classical statistics, humans had to do all the work. In machine learning and modern AI, the computers do.

It's not always the case, but when the engineers whom companies hide away in cubicle farms talk about machine learning, it's usually deep learning systems. These are the systems that use networks of artificial neurons that have more than three layers—and some have hundreds of thousands of them. Deep learning systems have proved to be so broadly applicable in so many situations that in 2024, the Nobel Prize in Physics was awarded to Geoffrey Hinton and John J. Hopfield for their work on neural networks.

On the same day that Hinton won the Nobel, I spoke with another "godfather" of AI, Yoshua Bengio, who in 2019 shared the Turing Award with Hinton and Yann LeCun for their work on neural networks.

"They changed the game in AI," said Bengio. "At a fundamental level, people used to think that, basically, to get intelligent machines you need to accumulate lots of knowledge and put that in machines. Whereas the point of view coming from physics they adopted is that there are some simple laws of physics that can be explained mathematically and give rise to intelligence in machines. That's what really excited me when I got into AI in 1985. That is still very powerful and at the heart of how we are doing AI now. But not in their days."

When Bengio said "not in their days," what he was referring to was the long, some might say dark, period in AI research when something called "symbolic reasoning" ruled the field. The general idea was that programmers should write down all the rules required to build an artificial intelligence, including all the relevant facts about the world. Neural networks were viewed as a backwater. At one point, the dean of the field of symbolic AI, Marvin Minsky, coauthored a book about why the original neural network, the Perceptron, could never be useful. That book, coupled with Minsky's sway over the field, held back neural network–based AI for decades and pushed those who would later be recognized as its pioneers to the periphery of academia, where they tinkered, often in obscurity.

But Hinton in Toronto, LeCun at New York University, and many other researchers in Europe and Japan soldiered on, building systems on shoestring budgets and proving concepts that would go on to make NVIDIA a trillion-dollar company, while scattering energy-hogging AI data centers all over the globe.

Which leads us back to Clorox wipes. Deep learning–based AI is what Clorox uses to predict demand for its products and plan accordingly. It's at the center of how the company does integrated business planning. And despite its utility, it's rare for companies to use it for this purpose. "Depending on who you ask, it's like five to seven percent of consumer and retail companies have deployed AI at scale for demand forecasting," said Rudy Colberg, the vice president of integrated business planning at Clorox. The company hired an outside consultancy to build a system to its specification, but it has the kind of engineering team maintaining and updating it that would be the envy of many tech startups. For example, the company's associate director of AI and machine learning has a PhD in computer science and artificial intelligence and spent nine years working as a manager of other engineers at Meta.

Clorox's planning AI enables the company to integrate many and varied streams of data. Like all deep learning systems, it's trained on this data, and within its artificial neural network, in the many hidden layers between its input and output layers, it creates an incomprehensibly tangled web of weighted connections that represents what it's learned from that data. This spaghetti of artificial neurons is the "black box" of AI, an indecipherable sea of values representing both an abstraction of the data that the AI has learned on and the "bag of heuristics"—that long list of rules of thumb—about what to do with it that I described in chapter 2.

One of the beautiful things about deep learning systems is that they can be fed arbitrarily large pools of data. There is an optimal ratio of data to connections in a neural network—in transformer-based AIs, it's about twenty tokens, or words, to every parameter or connection. Another thing that's great about deep learning AIs is that as prediction systems go, they are a kind of universal learner. They are able to handle any kind of data in which there is a relationship between one stream of information and another and to make sophisticated predictions based on those relationships.

For Clorox, using AI in its IBP means taking the usual streams of data you might throw into a demand-forecasting system—how much retailers have ordered in the past, how much they're actually selling—and adding some rather unusual ones. For example, the company uses long-term weather forecasting data to predict future demand for its Kingsford charcoal. And for predicting demand for its disinfectants and cleaners, it throws in data on the incidence of colds and flu in the United States that is gathered and distributed by the Centers for Disease Control and Prevention (CDC).

Still, most of the utility that Clorox derives from its machine learning–based demand prediction system comes from the fact that it's better at making predictions than the old system, which was purely statistics based. In August 2024, Clorox rolled out its AI-based prediction system across all of its North American business units. "The degree of improvement that we've seen in our forecasts has been very significant and has been incredibly valuable," said Rudy. Demand-planning work that once typically took six to eight weeks now takes just a few days, and the result is a demand forecast for not just every product but every variant of every product that Clorox makes.

It's not as if Clorox has handed its entire IBP process over to AI. Once the system has done its work of predicting demand based on all the data it's fed—much of it direct sales data from retailers—the sales and marketing teams at the company layer their own insights onto it, based on all the other knowledge they've gained from the real world, including conversations with retail buyers. The Achilles' heel of machine learning—or what I call classical AI, even though that might mean something else to a die-hard historian of the field—has always been that its predictions about the future are only as good as its data about the past. Predictive AI can interpolate based on past trends, but it's not very good at extrapolating that data to future ones that might be outside of its experience.

To be fair, humans aren't very good at this, either. But when things such as a global pandemic happen, we're at least capable of reasoning—as Clorox's sales team did at the time—that the demand for disinfectants and cleaning products was about to go through the roof. Big disjunctions, in which the relationships between existing variables change profoundly and move far outside of historical norms, tend to break traditional AI systems.

The Sixteenth Law of AI:
"Classic" predictive AI is brittle
and breaks when big changes occur.

The time saved by using a machine learning system to make predictions about demand enables Rudy's team to collect and add the subjective knowledge they've gathered. "Now the team is freed up to improve the forecast with all of those insights, and what has been great for us is the starting point that AI provides," he said. "Not only does the AI do it way faster than what we used to manage, but it is also much more accurate and has a greater richness of insight than anything like we used to have."

The speed of the system also enables the teams using it to ask "What if?" questions. What if, for example, there's another pandemic? Or the marketing team finds that generative AI has made ads for a particular product perform better? What if a TikTok about a celebrity's love of ranch dressing suddenly goes viral? Because IBP includes data not only about sales but also about marketing and other factors, it allows the teams to decide where to allocate resources as all of those things change.

At the end of the day, the goal of this system is to make sure that retailers get as much product as they want, without Clorox having to hold extra inventory to meet their orders. "It's absolutely delivering on those core, basic metrics," said Eric. "The AI is much better than people, both in terms of efficiency, in that it can think faster and predict the future better, but also in terms of cleaning up our processes. So we no longer get in a room and argue about whether we think Walmart's going to need x million whatever because the Walmart team has a different prediction than somebody else inside our headquarters building."

THE OGs OF WORKADAY AI

It's not just manufacturers who are transitioning from purely statistical methods to deep learning AI. My favorite example of this phenomenon will forever be insurance actuaries. Before we had predictive analytics, they managed to build an entire industry on the mathematics of predicting the future using nothing but statistics.

An insurer wants to know, given a set of facts about you, the odds that you'll die in the next ten years, get into a car accident, or be the owner of a home that will be damaged. While scientists and software engineers have all been heavy users of statistics, it's insurers that have been the most avid users of it to predict the future.

David MacInnis has a PhD in physics, and his dissertation was on statistical mechanics—one of the fields that Hinton and Hopfield borrowed from in their pioneering and Nobel Prize–winning work on neural networks. But his first job out of university wasn't at a tech company—at least not a conventional one. In 2008, he went to work for Allstate, the nearly century-old insurer that was originally part of Sears, Roebuck and Co.

In 1982, Hopfield, who would go on to share the Nobel with Hinton, came up with the idea of what would come to be known as Boltzmann machines. They were an important step in the evolution of neural nets and represent the stage at which ideas from statistical physics—precisely what MacInnis had received a PhD in—were imported into the mathematics underlying modern AI.

In 2007, David's expertise could have gotten him a job in academia but not in tech. At the time, few tech companies had any use for his skills. DeepMind, a London-based startup whose successes eventually led to the takeover of tech companies by deep neural networks, wasn't founded by Demis Hassabis and others until 2010. And Hinton didn't join Google until 2013.

At Allstate, however, David found a home as an associate predictive modeler. Predictive modeling is the use of statistics to predict the future. Its limitations are myriad—infamously, overreliance on it was one reason the 2008 financial crisis happened, when the models used to assure investors that the highest-rated bonds were safe proved woefully inadequate.

"Insurers have used prediction algorithms before anyone," said David. "Other companies know the price of their product. That is not the case for insurance; you are selling this policy to a consumer, and some individuals have no losses and others have a significant amount. Trying to price for that can be daunting."

For decades, insurers used statistical models to do this. As more and more data and computing power became available, they became more sophisticated, and insurers started using machine learning systems based on a variety of techniques. Then along came modern AI. Suddenly insurers could price policies based not only on how risky an individual was but the likelihood they'd buy the policy at a given price. Then insurers figured out that they could gather data on people's driving habits through a GPS-tracking app on their cell phones or a dongle they plugged into the data port in their car. "Before, we typically leveraged information like age, gender, and marital status, and that's how we typically priced you," said David. "We are now moving into this world where it can be more personalized based on your driving habits, and we can segment people based on that GPS information."

Because his is an industry that's already so comfortable with all the flavors of discriminative AI and machine learning, insurance companies are pouring those abilities into every part of how they interact with customers. If someone gets into an accident, they can take pictures of the damage and give their account of what happened. Their words will be translated into text with a proprietary AI, that text will be parsed by another AI known as a natural language processing system, and that data will be combined with photos of the damage, which will be processed by an image recognition system. Allstate can then begin the claims process automatically, before a human adjuster even looks at all of the information.

"We can get the consumer to tell us the story, and from there we can begin to make predictions based on 'Is it a total loss or not?' and determine what is the right kind of human adjuster for that. There are probably twenty different machine learning models in production just at that initial loss. A consumer may not even call us—they can start a claim through our quick photo claim through our mobile app, and then they submit pictures and maybe the consumer may never talk to a rep of ours," said David.

The systems are trained on the millions of claims Allstate handles every year and the communication between its employees and its customers about those claims. Allstate patents dozens of these innovations every year—the company filed sixty-six patent applications in 2024 alone—and one in ten are related to AI. "Estimating a cost to repair a damaged item without physically inspecting the item," an application filed in 2023, is instructive. It describes a system that matches an image sent by a user to a series of images depicting an ever-more-damaged item, and then "an estimated cost to repair the damaged item is generated based, at least in part, on the image selected." Another, filed in 2024, has a title that speaks for itself: "Generating insurance quotes." It describes a system that completely automates the process of selling insurance—down to generating a final quote.

Ironically, during a period of widespread layoffs in the tech industry, David now finds himself able to hire from the very tech companies that once shunned the kind of AI he—and researchers such as Hopfield and Hinton—specialize in.

Generative AI has taken off because it is, in a sense, the people's AI. Chatbots, as well as tools that can work with unstructured data and be directed with natural language, enable all of us to use AI in a way that's direct and intuitive. But classical AI, which requires huge amounts of structured data and the skills of data scientists and other experts, remains the backbone of countless systems and much of what we take for granted about how the internet and our modern world works. Its adoption remains slow in comparison to that of generative AI, precisely because it's difficult to get right and requires significant investment and expertise.

Perhaps in the future generative AI will make it easier to build systems with other, older forms of AI. Already, generative AI-based coding assistants are helping. The one thing they can't give us is the massive amounts of data that classical AI requires—and that is the difference between companies that can leverage it to build useful new products and a moat around their business and those that can't. "We are an insurance company, but at the end of the day we are a data and analytics company," said David.

In the next chapter, we're going to dive into an area where generative AI is doing things that no company using previous generations of AI imagined would be possible: coming up with new ideas.

TERMS

"Classic" AI: To computer scientists steeped in the field, this denotes a really old kind of AI, known as symbolic AI. But for our purposes, "classic" AI—aka AI classic—is everything that came before generative AI.

Integrated business planning: A technique of predicting the demand for the things a manufacturer makes and deciding how, when, and where to meet it by quantifying and taking into account everything that might influence all inputs and outcomes.

Predictive AI or predictive analytics: AI used to predict the future, based on the past. Traditionally, this was accomplished with statistical techniques, such as predictive modeling.

Discriminative AI: Closely related to predictive AI and predictive analytics. The canonical example is image recognition algorithms: Is this a picture of a cat or not? Discriminative AI is about determining whether something is one sort of thing or another, rather than generating an image or the next word in a sentence, as generative AI does.

Machine learning: A subset of AI, although these days people are more likely to speak in a way that implies the opposite now that AI has become so closely associated with deep learning systems and deep neural networks. Machine learning doesn't have to be based on neural networks at all; there are many algorithms that can achieve some sort of "learning," and researchers are constantly coming up with new ones.

Boltzmann machines: An early kind of neural network. Geoffrey Hinton and John J. Hopfield won the 2024 Nobel Prize in Physics for their work on these and subsequent artificial neural networks.

Deep learning: The foundational breakthrough that led to modern AI and eventually to the transformer models that made possible large language models. Deep learning systems are at their core deep neural networks, which means they are networks with hundreds, even hundreds of thousands, of layers of neurons. As in the human brain, this depth is essential to how these networks operate, because it's in the vast network of artificial neurons in the middle of these systems that information and rules for how to manipulate it are stored. While the number of researchers who initially developed deep neural networks was at first small, figuring out how to build and train modern deep learning systems has involved decades of fiddling and experimentation by thousands of researchers.

Symbolic AI: The idea, now largely fallen by the wayside, that the best way to build AI was for humans to explicitly program all the rules and knowledge it required.

SUMMARY

What to Know

AI classic, old-school AI, pregenerative AI, predictive AI, and discriminative AI are all broad terms for the many flavors of AI that predate the craze brought on by image generators and ChatGPT. After the introduction of transformer-based AI, even slightly older techniques such as deep learning were swiftly relegated to a sort of before times, especially as those trumpeting the newest kinds of generative AI declared that they were on a path to becoming human level in their abilities.

How to Think About It

When we talk about AI having a profound impact on our society, we are still talking, for the most part, about pregenerative AI. It's harder to implement, but in the right applications, it can be far more powerful than the kind of AI that's now in vogue. Making it work requires data and expertise. It's possible that in the future, generative AI will make it easier to create classical AI, but nothing currently on the horizon will change the need for a great deal of high-quality data in order to make AI work.

What Questions to Ask

Is a given AI system based on generative AI? If not, what kind of AI is it based on? Is it a deep learning system or some other form of machine learning? Where does the data it's trained on come from? Is the data labeled by humans, or can the system parse the data on its own? (In other words, is it a supervised or unsupervised learning system or some variant of those two broad categories?) If the builder of a tool can't or won't answer these questions, why not?

8

AI FOR INNOVATION

When, millennia from now, archaeologists dig through the layers of our current era—past traces of our efforts to cool the planet with sulfate aerosols, under the radioactive dust tossed off by tactical nukes, and below the parched soil of the second dust bowl—they will find fossilized in our trash heaps the packaging of something that historians will mark as a turning point in our history: the toilet bomb.

What will make the toilet bomb exceptional in the minds of future historians is that it was, so far as my research on this topic has been able to discern, the first mass-market product invented by AI. All subsequent economic upheavals brought about by, or wars fought with, intelligent machines may be traced to the time when we began to hand over that most human of activities—invention—to our AI companions.

In 2023, Clorox dominated the market for cleaning America's toilets. But being the category leader in toilet tablets, toilet wands, and squeeze bottle toilet cleaner was not enough. Like the polar explorers of the nineteenth century, the company's innovation team grew restless and sought new frontiers to conquer. The company's existing process for coming up with new ideas and testing them with consumers, which it calls its Discovery Process, worked well enough but took months. And people can come up with only so many new ideas for how to clean a toilet.

Enter AI. "We started working with generative AI systems to try and predict, what are the kinds of features we might innovate on in this space?" said Eric Schwartz.

Because the company already had a multistep discovery process for coming up with new products and qualifying them for market, adding AI to the mix was not simply a matter of asking ChatGPT for fresh ideas. Rather, at each stage of the company's existing discovery process, team members figured out a variety of ways generative AI could help speed things up. The result: The time required to generate a viable idea went from months to weeks.

The toilet bomb was the first successful example of this new, AI-enhanced process of invention and innovation. Clorox now uses this process to develop *all* of its new products, said Eric.

A TOILET BOMB FOR THE MIND

To understand what Clorox is doing, it helps to take a step back and ask: What do we know about using AI as a teammate to help generate new ideas? As it turns out, it's already quite a lot.

In the summer of 2024, when the world's first AI reasoning model, from OpenAI, was brand new, a posse of academics from Harvard Business School and the Wharton School conducted the world's first large-scale double-blind study of how AI can help both individuals and teams brainstorm new ideas. Their subjects were two sets of experts from the consumer products giant Procter & Gamble: commercial experts who were wise in the humanities-centered disciplines focused on identifying and addressing consumers' needs and technical R&D experts whose skills lay in coming up with new innovations in the lab. Those experts were generally well practiced at their arts, with on average more than ten years of experience.

The study looked at the ability of individuals and teams—with and without the help of AI chatbots—to come up with new products. It also examined the kinds of ideas they concocted. The results were unequivocal: Adding a chatbot to a daylong brainstorming and innovation process that required the experts to come up with a new product, its packaging, and strategies for selling it led to significantly better ideas, as rated by other humans. Intriguingly, the number of ideas rated as being in the top 10 percent skyrocketed with the addition of AI to a team.

An AI paired with an individual performed nearly identically with a two-person team (which always performs better than individuals on their own), suggesting that AI can sometimes be a substitute for a living, breathing, thinking partner, at least in that limited context. Finally, the use of AI helped commercial experts come up with solutions that were more technical and technical R&D experts come up with ideas that were more like those of their touchy-feely counterparts who were good at the quasianthropological work of addressing consumers' needs.

Despite that promising work, first published in early 2025, in all my reporting I've found only one real-world example of companies actually implementing this sort of thing in their day-to-day brainstorming and innovation pipelines: Clorox.

FROM SCOURING THE INTERNET TO SCOURING A TOILET

Clorox's new discovery process, which it calls "modernized discovery," is seeded with a vast corpus of ideas from the company's customers. The company uses a platform called Profitero+ to ingest ratings and reviews on its products from more than forty publicly accessible retailers and forums, including reviews on Amazon, Walmart, Target, and the like. This is part of a larger system the company calls Voice of the Consumer, which provides the team with a direct pipeline to unvarnished consumer feedback on a scale far grander than traditional focus groups provide.

"We learn what benefits actually resonate with consumers versus those that don't necessarily resonate with consumers," said Nicole Thomas. From 2024 to 2025, the company's data science team added generative AI capabilities to its Voice of the Consumer tool, allowing it to analyze online reviews and summarize what it finds. In addition, the company uses something called attribute-based sentiment analysis, which tells Nicole's team the resonance of various product attributes based on consumer mentions and average sentiment.

For example, what matters to consumers more when it comes to Burt's Bees lip balm, its ability to moisturize or its scent? "It's always scent," said Nicole. How does she know? Because a generative AI–summarized sentiment analysis of hundreds or even thousands of recent online reviews says so.

Knowing what consumers value gives the innovation team a starting point for thinking about enhancements to existing products. It can also be the seed of ideas for entirely new ones. That's how the company's generative AI–enhanced, internet-scouring voice of the consumer tool gave the toilet-cleaning team some new ideas about what consumers might respond to. "Foaming, for example, and colored foam came up as something consumers chattered about," said Eric. "There were small early products that went in that direction and offered that feature, which the consumer rated highly on Amazon or Reddit. And so it came on our radar screen because of our generative AI tools."

Feeding that insight and data to a frontier AI model primes the model with some knowledge about what consumers might want. Then you just start asking it for ideas. The company is model agnostic and uses a variety of AI chatbots. "You can go in there and prompt it with 'I'm a toilet-cleaning product manufacturer, give me ten ideas for what I should launch,' and ChatGPT will do it for you," said Eric.

The idea of a "toilet bomb" came out of one such session with

AI. "A toilet bomb was counterintuitive to us," said Eric. "Machine ideas are usually a little bit crazy. We might get ten ideas from AI and pick the two that make us say, 'Actually, well, those are really intriguing. Those might work.'" The key to making this approach work is providing the AI with as much context as possible—for example, the distillation of all the consumer sentiment Clorox gathers from all over the internet. Once again, the Ninth Law of AI—Context is king—asserts itself.

The team took a couple of ideas from the AI, a couple from the humans brainstorming with one another and the AI, and refined them all in an ongoing dialog with the context-informed chatbot. The result was a handful of new ideas with better-than-average scores in tests with consumers, generated much more quickly than in the past.

Given the limitations of large language models, this sequence might seem like a daft way to use one to help come up with new ideas. After all, if large language models are more akin to something doing an approximate search of its internet-size memories than something capable of true reasoning, much less creativity and ideation, how can they possibly have good ideas? It helps to recall that when we are having a conversation with an AI, what we are really doing is pushing it through progressively farther flung reaches of its vector database. In the context of that vast library of Babel containing every text on the open internet, the transcripts of countless hours of YouTube videos and podcasts, patents and legal documents, chats and forum posts, essays and confessions and news articles and books, we are asking it to combine words and concepts in ways that might be novel. This process works, when it does, because our *prompts* and the data we are feeding the AI are novel.

I was once deeply skeptical of the idea that AI could possibly be a thought partner in coming up with new ideas that were any good. But then I met Ethan Mollick, a business professor at the Wharton School who has become a globe-trotting adviser on AI strategy to countless companies.

There is a certain vibe to AI leaders, and Mollick fits right in with this group. I've met many of them, including Sam Altman, the Taiwanese businessman Kai-Fu Lee, Demis Hassabis, and Yann LeCun, and interviewed far more, including Zoox CEO Aicha Evans, Cohere Vice President of Research Sara Hooker, Marc Benioff, and Microsoft AI CEO Mustafa Suleyman. Mollick fits the type: winsome, hypercurious, a little mischievous. In a field this demanding, this new, and this quickly developing, its leaders are people who have built into their personality a high degree of optimism and an almost childlike curiosity.

Over the course of a leisurely stroll through Wharton's campus on a warm spring day, Ethan and I discussed what he had discovered not only through obsessive use of ChatGPT and its competitors but also through incorporating it into the courses in entrepreneurship that he teaches.

Ethan's conclusion, after exploring the applications of generative AI in education and business development, is that there needs to be "one of me in every field"; that is, someone who devotes as much of their time and energy as he does to plumbing the depths of the vast, alien AI systems we've created. Only an expert in medicine, in law, in finance, in any field you can think of can come to understand what he calls the "jagged frontier" of AI, the uneven boundary between what it's capable of today and what tasks are left for humans to pick up.

In his courses, Ethan discovered that students who used AI to help them come up with new ideas weren't just coming up with more of them; they actually seemed to be better ideas. As he has written, "Despite of (or in fact, because of) all its constraints and weirdness, [generative AI] is perfect for idea generation."

Research has shown that idea generation benefits from differences among those in a group coming up with ideas, including diversity in backgrounds, core beliefs, and social networks, all of which can bring new ideas to the table and spark novel ones. "AI is not a substitute for this," he added, "but it is a way of adding extreme difference and even weirdness to your idea generation sessions that can be useful to build on."

So he started to research the subject at actual companies. In the summer of 2024, he teamed up with a few other researchers to conduct the gold standard of scientific studies, a randomized, controlled trial on a large number of subjects. Their experiment included 776 professionals at Procter & Gamble. His team conducted one-day workshops in which they had to develop new product ideas, packaging, and retail strategies for the parts of the business they worked in and then submit their ideas to management. Half of the participants were given GPT-4 to work with, and the other half had to do it the old-fashioned way. Individuals were further divided up into teams and solo innovators.

Unsurprisingly, teams outperformed individuals. But surprisingly, individuals who used AI did just as well as teams without AI. "This suggests that AI effectively replicated the performance benefits of having a human teammate—one person with AI could match what previously required two-person collaboration," he concluded.

In at least one study, AI came up with better ideas than unaided MBA students did on its own. "Generative AI has brought a new source of ideas to the world," wrote the researchers. "It doesn't matter if you are working on a pitch for your local business-plan competition or if you are seeking a cure for cancer— every innovator should develop the habit of complementing his or her own ideas with the ones created by technology."

The Seventeenth Law of AI:
AI isn't creative, but it can help you be.

Let's get back to Clorox's toilet bomb. It's an odd concept—the sort of thing that might come out of the random and offbeat noise that large language models can throw off. "A toilet bomb was sort of a mash-up of categories that we were already in," said Eric, the company's CMO. "It went into the bowl, not the tank, and foamed up, and then you scrubbed as well. It's something that was generated by the AI, and frankly, the language was as well. Calling it a toilet 'bomb,' that was a little bit counterintuitive for the brains behind a toilet-cleaning manufacturer."

Of course, once you have a concept, you still need to generate assets to go with it: packaging, the design of the thing itself, images of it in action. Using generative AI in this process leads to a system the Clorox product team calls "digital prototyping." Here, too, AI chatbots and image generators greatly speed up the process. Need some quick art to depict what would happen if you were to drop a hot pink bath bomb into your toilet?

Me, to ChatGPT: "Please render a photorealistic image of what the results would be if I dropped a hot pink bath bomb into my toilet."

ChatGPT, moments later: a photorealistic image of a toilet bowl full of an almost violently pink foam, a sphere like a bath bomb bubbling at its center.

Need some quick marketing copy to go with it? Here's what Google Gemini spat out: "Tired of scrubbing? Toss in Toilet Grenade! This revolutionary cleaner erupts with powerful foam, blasting away stains and leaving your toilet sparkling fresh. Simply drop, fizz, and flush for effortless cleaning. Experience the explosive power of clean!"

Say what you will about how AI is destroying our ability to come up with new ideas on our own, but that description, on the back of a box of "Toilet Grenade," would 100 percent convince me to at least try it, if only to share a video of the results with the group chat.

The Eighteenth Law of AI:
AI can't create finished products, but it's great at quickly generating digital prototypes.

Digital prototype in hand, the team can now start testing the idea on real people. This process is called concept testing. An old technique, it's traditionally conducted in small, in-person focus groups. In the past, this required months of effort and gathering people in person, with people on product teams flying about the country and staying in hotels for days as they convened and oversaw focus groups. Afterward, it took days to process the resulting notes and transcripts.

Nowadays, Clorox takes its digital prototypes and floats them on social media, said Michael Ott. Putting product ideas and accompanying pictures up on the company's various feeds produces quick feedback from a huge pool of potential customers. "Ten thousand consumers can start weighing in on these things and saying, 'Oh, that's a cool idea' and 'Oh, have you thought about this as well?'" he told me. In the old days, coming up with new concepts and modifying them based on customer feedback could take months, but with quick feedback from the internet and digital prototyping, the amount of time that process requires can be cut in half.

It's not as if AI is coming up with final product designs, says Michael. But it can get companies down the path of figuring out something that will actually help consumers much more quickly. "AI gets you maybe seventy-five percent of the way there. And then our team, who is experienced in CPG and the strategies of

Walmart and the journey that we're on with our brands and things like that, takes it the last twenty-five percent of the way and makes it something great."

It wasn't just the weirdness of a toilet bomb and its novelty that made it appealing. In tandem, the humans and AI working in the company's modernized discovery process had managed to hit on a mechanism and associations that appealed to consumers. Why wouldn't you "bomb" a filthy toilet with a cleaning product that, because it foams and turns the water an industrial bright color rarely found in nature, appears to be doing so much more than just dissolving? Consumers felt that the product was in some sense automating part of the onerous job of scrubbing a toilet. And the team succeeded at bringing a little bit of joy to a job that no one likes to do. The toilet bomb was, said Eric, a "sweet spot" of traits that the innovation team never would have come up with without the help of AI at several steps in their discovery process.

Using AI as part of the discovery process also meant that it went much quicker. Typically, consumer products companies can spend years developing a new product. But the toilet bomb went from a pitch to retailers' loading docks in just three months.

Making this AI-driven discovery process the norm across the company has also tripled the number of ideas in the company's innovation pipeline, said Michael. That means the company has more ideas it can say no to and can be more selective about what it brings to market.

One thing that's important to think about when evaluating all of the studies and anecdotes about how AI can lead to more and better ideas: This process is, by necessity, anchored by what the AI thinks are good ideas. (See chapter 4 for more on what anchoring is and why it's something to be wary of.)

Right now, AIs are evolving very quickly. OpenAI, for example, is working hard on a model that is particularly good at creative writing, and the new abilities will be part of its mainstream model by the time you read this. Claude has, in the past, been lauded for its creativity and writing abilities. The focus of the team behind Gemini has been reducing hallucinations, which tends to trade off with creativity. What's more, all of these models are increasingly customizable by developers using them for their own purposes. Want a more "creative" thought partner? It's possible to fine-tune ChatGPT to behave that way, but only if you're a developer paying for the kind of access developers need to white-label a chatbot and incorporate it into their systems.

What this means is that there is a wide variety of AIs providing different responses to the same prompts. But given the dominance of ChatGPT, if two different companies use similar prompts when asking it for new ideas, the odds are that there will be some overlap in its responses to the companies—and neither would ever know unless they both brought the same ChatGPT-inspired product to market.

One way we know about this consistency of responses is that it's become a problem among developers using AI chatbots to write code. Security researchers have found that when AI coding assistants hallucinate a particular and important reference in code—to other libraries of code—they frequently make up the same code library again and again. This has led to a potential vulnerability in "vibe-coded" applications made with AI, where hackers can create the made-up libraries of code referenced in the AI-produced programs and fill them with malicious code.

All of these issues are, in some ways, unavoidable. They arise because of underlying tensions among the needs of different users of AI chatbots. Many users of AI chatbots want them to provide consistent responses. But people using them for creativity might want them to be looser and more random in their responses. The takeaway is that as we incorporate AIs into our creative processes, it's important to be skeptical of overreliance on them to come up with new ideas—because they might be offering the same ideas to our competitors.

○ TERMS

Sentiment analysis: The use of a kind of AI known as natural language processing to determine the emotional tone of language.

The "jagged frontier" of AI: A concept invented by the AI enthusiast and expert Ethan Mollick, a professor of entrepreneurship and related fields at the Wharton School. It describes the uneven boundary between what AI is good at and what it's not good at.

Digital prototyping: The process of using generative AI to come up with the text and visuals that depict a new tool or product.

SUMMARY

What to Know

Brainstorming new ideas works best when it's a team sport. Absent other humans to practice it with, AI can be a good substitute. Structured systems for coming up with new ideas can use many kinds of generative AI throughout the process in a number of different ways.

How to Think About It

From systems for writing new songs to methods for brainstorming new ideas, people have long used various techniques to spark creativity. AI is yet another one and unique in that it can generate ideas on its own. In innovation, more than any other field, an AI is only as good as the humans using it and the human-built scaffolding that surrounds it.

What Questions to Ask

If AI is supposed to become part of a process for coming up with new ideas, products, tools, or lines of business, how will your company measure its impact, compared with the process of unaided ideation? How can the process of innovation be broken into steps, and how can different kinds of generative AI be incorporated into each of them? How will you ensure that humans are the ultimate and unbiased judges of the ideas that result from this hybrid process?

9

TAKE YOUR AI AGENT
TO WORK DAY

Founded in 1969 in Dallas, the family-owned construction company Rogers-O'Brien builds big multistory structures in Texas—everything from a gigantic spacecraft garage in Boca Chica for SpaceX to the sprawling 433,540-square-foot headquarters and corporate campus of Pizza Hut in Plano. The company has about seventy different major construction projects in progress at any one time and booked close to $1.2 billion in revenue in 2024, making it one of the fifty biggest builders in the country. In a state whose construction projects tend to favor quantity over quality, Rogers-O'Brien focuses on the latter, as evidenced by the contracts it's won for high-performance structures such as data centers, pharmaceutical labs, and the specialized factories for semiconductors called fabs.

Todd Wynne is the chief innovation officer of Rogers-O'Brien, a role that combines those of chief information officer, chief technology officer, and chief of whatever you might call a skunkworks for the construction industry.

And boy, does his industry need to innovate. Construction is unique among industries in that productivity per unit of input—labor, materials, dollars—has actually *declined* over the past fifty years. A construction worker on the job today is less productive than one rolling up to a job site sporting a cop mustache and blasting Three Dog Night in 1970. Contrast that with manufacturing in the United States, where productivity grew by 2.1 percent on average between 1947 and 2018.

In other words, over the same period that productivity in manufacturing *went up* by a factor of nine, productivity in construction *declined* by more than a third. The failure of the construction industry to become any more efficient in the past half century is so bad that it's a drag on the entire U.S. economy. Researchers have called the long-term doldrums U.S. construction finds itself in "stunningly bad productivity performance for a major sector."

This isn't just about some abstract impact on America's collective wealth—although, considering that the U.S. construction sector is almost as big as the automobile industry, it's not trivial. The industry's failure to become more productive is a major reason why the United States has a housing crisis.

The productivity challenge in construction is one reason why, paradoxically, Todd likes his job. Speaking with the subtle twang of a man who never left his home state, he rhapsodizes about the ways in which technology is helping Rogers-O'Brien do things in a better way. But he also laments that one reason he has to push the adoption of AI is that a quarter of the nation's construction workers are over fifty-five years of age, and with retirement approaching, they can't pass on their knowledge fast enough.

"Our industry right now is going through its digital transformation, whereas every other industry has already gone through it," he said. But that's just the first reason construction is one of the most interesting case studies in AI. The second is that construction, like manufacturing, is an inherently conservative, risk-averse discipline on account of the high cost of screwing things up. Then there are the brutal physical realities of construction, which an industry insider once described to me as being akin to manufacturing a car in a muddy field. And because the industry has resisted change for so long, its overdue technological transformation is now happening at the same time as the rollout of practical, accessible AI. Thus, in some ways, the construction industry has the opportunity to leapfrog others that have benefited from AI but are burdened by legacy IT systems.

The final reason construction is such a fascinating case study is that all this digital transformation is colliding with a whole other set of big—and urgent—changes to the materials and methods used in the industry. Builders have spent decades attempting to make structures more energy efficient. Along the way, they accidentally developed systems people seem to care about even more. Techniques that were once the domain of high-performance builders have trickled out into the mainstream. Buildings are called upon to do things they've never had to do before, such as maintaining occupants' mental and physical health, while also being defenses against the ever more extreme and varied weather our planet is throwing at us. New techniques and materials pioneered for Leadership in Energy and Environmental Design (LEED), WELL Building, and Passive House standards are just beginning to see widespread adoption. All of this is informed by the rapidly advancing field of "building science"—a discipline both ancient and in some ways quite new, having existed in its modern form only since the energy crisis of the 1970s.

The simple facts of geography and humans' intense desire to customize the places in which we live, work, and gather mean that there is no silver bullet for the construction industry—nothing that can transform it the way the assembly line transformed manufacturing. No amount of prefabrication, automation, or building-scale 3D printing can sweep away all of the industry's problems and constraints. Most buildings remain stubbornly bespoke. But that doesn't mean they don't also have elements, themes, and best practices that are repeatable across projects—exactly the sort of thing that modern deep learning systems and generative AI can help with.

"Every building we build is a prototype," said Todd. "It's a new design, a new schedule, new materials, a new team. In North America, owners do not like their buildings looking like their competitors'." The dream, he continued, would be if all of the fuzzy, human, tribal knowledge that building managers and the up to fifty different companies that come together to work on a Rogers-O'Brien structure could be preserved across projects and made easily accessible to the fresh mix of people and contractors who come together for the next building.

This is, as you've no doubt gathered by this point in the book, exactly the sort of knowledge management problem at which modern transformer- and large language model–based AIs excel. And so Rogers-O'Brien uses a number of kinds of AI to make its projects run more smoothly, keep everyone on the same page, and organize the sequential and parallel work of hundreds of workers.

The company's central system of truth and coordination on any given project is a cloud-based service called Procore. The best way to describe Procore for those unfamiliar with enterprise software is: Imagine Microsoft 365—that is, all of Microsoft's primary productivity programs—but for construction companies. For those familiar with the deeper reaches of corporate IT systems, comparables would be Salesforce, SAP, Asana, or Jira—but for construction. Procore Technologies isn't alone in its industry— the software giant Autodesk has a Construction Cloud offering that is its main competitor—but by virtue of having been around and growing steadily over the past twenty years, it's one of the most dominant platforms in its niche, with more than a billion dollars in annual revenue.

Since about 2020, Procore has been adding AI features at a steady clip. It started with systems to help builders automatically estimate the amount of materials and labor they'd need, a process called takeoff. In 2023, the company announced a product called

Copilot, an across-the-board assistant like the one that Microsoft has crammed into everything it offers.

Procore now uses, on the back end, large language models from OpenAI, Google, and others, just like every other model-agnostic software company making AI genuinely useful by making it a feature, rather than a product unto itself. (Recall the Third Law of AI from chapter 1: AI is a feature, not a product.)

Rajitha Chaparala is a vice president at Procore, heading up its data and AI efforts. Previously, she was a leader in insurance and then financial services, doing credit analytics, which gave her experience in the two industries that were by far the earliest adopters of machine learning.

Starting around 2019, Procore began hiring people with backgrounds in analytics, machine learning, and, later on, computer vision. This kind of expertise has proved to be applicable in everything Procore does, which begins the moment that an architect hands off the drawings for a building.

The first phase is called preconstruction, and it begins with what is essentially an audit of the drawings created by an architect and then a process of refining them into something a general contractor such as Rogers O'Brien and its many subcontractors can use to realize a building.

This is a journey I know all too well. Throughout the writing of this book, my spouse and I oversaw the construction of a modest studio space for her work, beginning with the demolition of the rotting, century-old hulk of an oversize shed it replaced. The project was handled by a friend and neighbor who owns a small construction company. They do great work, but in the old style. At every stage of the process, we talked through what was going on, how it would be accomplished, and how it might be enhanced by AI or at least a degree of digital transformation. Through no fault of my very capable friend, at no point in the process were we able to figure out how AI could be incorporated into the way his team worked. It was an ongoing object lesson in why the entire construction industry is so resistant to advances that could increase its productivity.

One of the most important phases for all builders—and one that could most benefit from AI—is preconstruction. General contractors win only a fraction of the projects they bid on. When I talked to my friend and his construction manager about their primary challenges as a small firm, after the scarcity of labor in their industry, their inability to bid on more projects was the number one bottleneck to growing their business. For big construction companies, this is no less of a bottleneck. They may have more employees, but with an aging workforce, those with enough experience to accurately estimate the cost of a job are growing scarce. (One calculation found that workers in the construction industry are aging out so quickly that it could lose half of them by 2030.)

For us, preconstruction consisted of everyone involved eyeballing the drawings created by an architect. For Rogers-O'Brien, it begins with an AI tool such as Firmus, which bills itself as "Your AI ally in preconstruction clarity." While preconstruction involves many steps, one of the most important is transforming blueprints into more elaborate construction drawings and 3D models that try to account for every detail any construction crew might need to know about.

AN INDUSTRY STILL RUNNING ON PAPER

A totally bananas fact about the construction industry is how much of it still runs on PDFs. You would think, as I once did, that the entire field was now running on the architectural equivalent of CAD drawings—those incredibly fine-grained 3D plans that are used in manufacturing, to create injection molds for plastic parts, say, or as a specification for a metal part that will be milled out of a solid block. But no. Just as my friend's construction company started—and ended—their build of our small shed studio with a handful of printed-out pieces of paper, much of the construction industry relies on two-dimensional floor plans emailed from architect to builder as if we were all still living in the 1990s. This is an industry in which taking iPads onsite to view these documents is considered technologically advanced.

This leads to *a lot* of problems, starting with confusion about the precise 3D layout of the functional sculpture that construction workers are tasked with building. This is compounded by the fact that dozens of subcontractors representing various specializations and trades all have to come together, sequentially and in parallel, to get it done. So it's incumbent on the construction manager and the subcontractors' supervisors to be the decision makers and central sources of truth for all the fiddly details that inevitably come up. This dynamic is so common in construction that the process has been formalized and has a name, "request for information." When that doesn't work or it becomes apparent something has been overlooked, a "request for change" often follows.

The process of rework is so devastating to the productivity of anyone making a thing that there is an entire manufacturing discipline devoted to stamping it out completely, to ensure that things are made correctly the first time. In construction, avoiding it at every scale, from the overall design of a project to its smallest detail, is equally critical. Bent Flyvbjerg, a Danish academic and expert in why big infrastructure projects are so frequently delayed and go over budget, calls the good kind of construction management "Think slow, act fast," by which he means that the most important first step in making a project come out on time and on budget—surveys suggest that at least half do not—is an elaborate preplanning phase.

Firmus is a small tech startup built on the idea that AI can help automate the process of figuring out all that's missing or overlooked in the blueprints of a building. It was cofounded in 2019 by Shir Abecasis, a veteran of Israel's Unit 8200, where she worked on data analysis and cybersecurity. (Unit 8200 is the equivalent of the United States' National Security Agency [NSA] or Great Britain's Government Communication Headquarters [GCHQ] and is well known for its involvement in the Stuxnet computer worm attack on Iran's nuclear industry.) "I was always passionate about how you can sort of predict the future if you're using data correctly—it's like a superpower," she told me. She had no background in construction, but it was apparent to her that the planning phase of construction was an area in need of her skills.

Much rework in construction is due to starting with flawed or incomplete plans. And research suggests that 5 percent of the direct costs of an average construction project goes to rework, and on account of all the headaches involved, the total of direct and indirect costs is closer to 10 percent of a project's budget. One study found that up to 30 percent of the work done by crews is actually rework.

A common example of how bad design leads to rework is that a blueprint will specify that, for example, bathroom walls in a new apartment building should be painted, but an interior design brief shows that they should be tiled. If a contractor bidding on the project misses this discrepancy, it can mean a huge loss for it if it bids based on the assumption that the bathrooms will be painted, while missing the fact that its contract says they should be tiled. These kinds of issues have led to a growing cottage industry of preconstruction analysis firms and consultants; Shir figured it was a prime area for automation through AI.

Blueprints, which are drawn with a standard design language and set of symbols, are a prime application for machine vision and machine learning. Converting blueprints into structured data, which can then be queried with software, is step one. "An example I often give is 'Let's say I receive a drawing, and I want to look for doors that are fire rated for two hours but sit within walls that aren't fire rated, which is a problem,'" said Shir. "If I have an image in front of me, I can't ask the image."

It takes a human being twenty to forty hours to do a complete preconstruction review of typical blueprints for Rogers-O'Brien, said Todd, while Firmus's software does it more or less instantaneously. A human still has to review its work, but it means turning around a preconstruction analysis in forty-eight hours, versus the two to three weeks it used to take.

The entire point of a system such as Firmus's is that the AI becomes invisible. "That's the beauty of AI—people don't need to understand it at all," said Shir. "All that is happening in the back end, all of this structured data, it's invisible. It allows people to continue to do whatever they did before and to use the same language they've always used, and the machine can understand what they're asking for."

With traditional software—and this is as true in construction as in any other industry—the mode of interaction we've all become accustomed to is complexity. While Steve Jobs tried to make software accessible by developing a graphic user interface, the result has been a world that is only slightly less complicated than the realm of pure code that developers inhabit. Software has become more bloated, buttons shrink and multiply, workflows become increasingly complicated.

"Now, what AI is creating is a reality where people can ask questions in their own words and it understands what they're asking. For people in construction that's amazing, because when we first presented our software, they thought, 'Oh, great, I need to learn another piece of software.' But then they upload a project, and they get a report telling them all of the issues in their project, and this input-output behavior was a shock. The report we gave them was the same report they could get if someone ran the process for them manually."

Firmus's software is what, by any rational, outcome-based definition of the term, would be called agentic AI, even though it's not primarily transformer-based or generative AI. It ingests data and, with zero supervision, creates an elaborate set of outputs—primarily a dashboard and reports—that humans can then act on. Many systems built with AI chatbots and related technologies aspire to do this, with mixed results. But there are early indications that those who use chatbot-derived AI agents most successfully build and use them in precisely this way—more like robots on a factory assembly line than as assistants.

This might seem to fly in the face of previous chapters in this book about individual knowledge workers using AI as assistants. But that's the funny thing about modern AI, especially generative AI. Recall from chapter 1 that AI is what's known as a "general-purpose technology," like electricity or the automobile. And while many of us will use it as an assistant—will in time, I suspect, find it odd not to have near-constant access to AI assistants—the bulk of its use will be in systems in which it's just another form of automation.

Recently, Dustin Moskovitz, the Facebook cofounder and CEO of Asana, the cloud-based project management system, posted on Bluesky that he was seeing clear power laws in the adoption of Asana's AI features, which can be used to build AI agents.

What he meant was that a small number of organizations—and within those organizations a small number of users—were calling on AIs in the agent-based workflows they'd created far more than everyone else who used them, leading to a power law distribution in the use of the company's AI services. (A power law distribution looks like either exponential growth or exponential decay and could describe, for example, wealth distribution in the United States, where a tiny number of billionaires have tremendous amounts of it, the merely rich have far less, and most of us are out in the long, flat tail of wealth distribution.)

When I asked him what he thought the secret of those AI power users was, he said, "I think they know how to treat AI like a factory line instead of like an assistant." This, I realized, was the logical corollary of AI being used primarily as a feature within other software, rather than a product on its own, once that logic was applied to how AI is used in agents, where it becomes simply another cog in a machine.

The Nineteenth Law of AI:
Treat AI agents as robots on an assembly line
rather than as assistants.

In the not-too-distant past, treating AI as merely a service offered to developers was a recipe for financial disaster. The companies that offered developers access to their models so that they could be used as a part of some other service or function that might be used over and over again charged them on a per token basis.

But the cost of AI has diminished dramatically. When ChatGPT first debuted, it cost developers $20 for every million tokens—or words—they fed into it. The cost per million input tokens as of this writing, for a far better model, is now 10 cents. It's even less, just 2.5 cents, if developers reuse the same prompts and are content to get the answers they got the last time they used those prompts. This is the quantitative expression of the concept I referenced in chapter 2 that is driving adoption of AI across the board: what OpenAI's Sam Altman calls "intelligence too cheap to meter."

Microsoft CEO Satya Nadella has boiled this trend down to a pithy aphorism—or at least one that's pithy if you're familiar with the history of manufacturing. "What Lean did for manufacturing, AI will do for knowledge work," he said in the keynote speech of Microsoft's 2024 conference for developers and IT pros. "It's all about increasing value and decreasing waste."

Lean is the manufacturing discipline I mentioned earlier, which is all about eliminating rework in goods coming off the assembly line. If we extend Satya's analogy to some of the other features of Lean, we should anticipate that one of the major drivers of the future use of frontier AI models will be the process of continuous improvement and refinement—known as *kaizen,* Japanese for "improvement"—which is one of the keys to Lean.

Many companies have tried to automate the takeoff process, in which a general contractor figures out the total cost of materials a building will require, with varying degrees of success. Procore can do it, and Autodesk has its own Takeoff software to extract this information, via a rules-based system, from the 2D and 3D models that designers and engineers construct in its building information management system. "When we get the drawings from the design team, we have to actually do takeoff measurements of how many linear feet of wall is there, so we can calculate how much paint or wallpaper or tile is going to be on there," said Todd. For this, Rogers-O'Brien is now turning to a new product called Togal.AI that, like Firmus's system, uses computer vision to analyze blueprints but, instead of examining them for completeness, calculates how much it will cost to realize them.

The founder and CEO of Togal.AI is former congressman Patrick E. Murphy, who represented Florida's 18th District for four years. The reason he founded an AI-focused construction services company in 2019, he told me, was that his dad owned a sizable construction business. "I grew up working in all aspects of the business, in the field and office," he said. After the Deepwater Horizon oil spill, he started an environmental cleanup company and spent time in the Florida Keys, working on recovery from that disaster. That motivated him to run for Congress, and after he served two terms, he returned to the family construction business.

"In 2017 and 2018, I realized that I'd been gone twelve years or so, and basically nothing had changed. I'm sure you've seen the stats on construction, but it's one of the most antiquated industries."

Patrick started going through the financials of his family's construction business and found that the single biggest piece of overhead for the company was its estimating department, and most of what that department did was takeoff estimates. He'd grown up doing those with his grandfather, using a ruler on paper, and in all the intervening time the only innovation had been that people had started doing it, still manually, on a computer with a mouse. At the time, no one else was trying to automate the task with AI, so he raised money and started hiring developers and AI experts. Togal.AI now has five thousand customers in thirty-two countries, including giants such as Clark Construction—and of course Rogers-O'Brien.

Togal.AI is a prime example of a topic we'll get into more in the final section of this book: what it takes to build your own AI and how doing so can enable your customers to do things that no other software is capable of. Doing this isn't easy, so it also creates a significant moat between a company like Togal.AI and any potential competitors.

To start, Patrick's employees had to procure a large amount of data that isn't exactly lying around on the internet. Then, because the company's machine vision system is based on deep learning and is a supervised learning system, they had to have experts label all the data. "It took us years to aggregate tens, and now over hundreds of thousands of plans, in all sorts of different languages and formats, and then label that data," he told me. "We tried to take shortcuts, and it didn't work. So we ended up hiring a team of twenty-five architects and engineers to do that data labeling in a very precise, consistent manner in order for our algorithms to process that at a level of accuracy that was going to hold up."

The "classic AI" I discussed in chapter 7 has remained the sole purview of companies with enough resources to build and maintain it precisely because of the challenges in feeding it enough of the right kind of data. "We had to be very focused on the data set, cleaning the data, organizing it, labeling it in a precise way, so the AI could actually learn. Being very targeted in what we were trying to do with it and building our own proprietary models and our own proprietary data set was very helpful."

Like Firmus, Togal.AI's system is the kind of AI agent that is essentially a robot on the factory floor of knowledge work. Both embody the law of AI as a feature: the importance of scaffolding and context, the need for high-quality data, the principle that AI is best applied to repetitive, tedious, and toilsome tasks, and its power to digest unstructured data—in this case, building plans instead of language.

Since their debut, almost all of the focus on AI agents has been about how they automate coding and back-office tasks. As we've seen in this chapter, those kinds of tasks are ubiquitous and can be bottlenecks to productivity in many of the industries we depend on for our most basic needs. But this discussion has been biased by the kinds of jobs that people who create software and write about it tend to have: desk jobs. In the next chapter, we'll get into the more than 60 million workers in the United States—and the billions worldwide—who don't work at desks and who stand to be impacted by AI in ways that previous generations of software couldn't accomplish.

○ **TERMS**

Digital transformation: A process of converting existing processes to a fully digital workflow, often used to describe subsequent generations of these transformations, that is, upgrades to existing digital technologies. Most of all, digital transformation is about changing workflows and ways of doing things to make them more efficient. One of the keys to the productivity gains of generative AI is that it facilitates digital transformation—that is, it makes it easier for individuals and organizations to make the workflow transformations they should have been doing anyway.

Tribal knowledge: The tacit knowledge passed from experts in an organization or field to their mentees, also known as institutional knowledge. Much of it is codified somewhere in the document repositories companies and individuals maintain, but finding it and making it usable can be next to impossible. A form of unstructured data that makes tribal or institutional knowledge accessible through a question-and-answer interface is one of the most obvious and best use cases for large language models, especially as their capacity for search and memorization of new information improves.

Lean manufacturing: A system of manufacturing pioneered by Toyota, built on minimizing waste and maximizing productivity. Microsoft CEO Satya Nadella has said that AI will do for knowledge work what Lean did for manufacturing, which leads to a number of helpful conclusions about how to think about AI and in particular AI agents—as cogs in larger machines or robots on an assembly line, rather than as autonomous workers or assistants.

SUMMARY
What to Know
AI agents are the flexible, machine learning, and machine vision-enhanced robots of the Information Age and represent an AI upgrade to traditional workflows.

How to Think About It
Picture a factory full of two kinds of robots. The first are traditional industrial robots—precise and indefatigable. They are able to perform the same action over and over—welding, painting, picking, and placing—but depend on consistency in the materials that arrive at their workstations. These are the physical manifestation of traditional software workflows. Now imagine a new kind of robot, with cameras, sensors, and just enough intelligence to be flexible in how it responds to its environment, like a Roomba or a Spot robot dog. This is the state of today's AI agents, which have some flexibility but are far from being truly autonomous.

What Questions to Ask
Under what circumstances does any given AI agent break? Has it been designed so that the conditions in which it fails are knowable? What user interface conventions make it easy for a human to check its work? How does the time spent dealing with the failures of an AI agent compare to the time saved when it successfully automates a task?

10

AI FOR DESKLESS
WORKERS

Discussions about the nature of work are biased by the kind of work that enables a person to pontificate on the subject. This can make it easy to miss the ways that AI, something we tend to think of as being most helpful to knowledge workers, can also transform the nature of work for others.

Estimates vary, but something like 63 percent of Americans work at a desk, meaning that the other 37 percent—factory workers, farmers, nurses and doctors, pilots, delivery drivers, teachers, cooks and waiters, retail salespeople, and construction workers—generally do not. They're what's known, somewhat unartfully, as "deskless" workers. Managing and communicating with construction workers, in particular, who don't work at the same place every day, can be especially difficult. Todd of Rogers-O'Brien compares it to herding cats.

Traditionally, everything from whether or not someone who goes onto a construction site has completed an orientation and safety training to the log of the hours workers spent onsite that day was all done on paper, and then those numerous pages would be collected by a site supervisor and scanned into a system such as Procore. All of this daily paperwork—which also includes forms such as those for establishing qualifications and handling inspections—ate close to a half an hour a day of each worker's time. And supervisors spent an inordinate amount of their time chasing down workers who hadn't filled out their paperwork for that day. "There was a huge administrative burden on supervisors for collecting the time sheets of employees coming onsite or making sure that they took the safety orientation," said Todd.

That was where the AI agents from a company called Nyfty.AI came in. All of the paperwork and communication that was once done by supervisors is now automated by an AI chatbot that every worker can access on their phone. And it's not an app; when workers arrive onsite, they scan a QR code, and all reporting from that point on takes place over text message. The dozens of different tasks that supervisors used to have to handle in person with as many different forms are now channeled through a chatbot that's accessible from every worker's pocket.

What's more, these agents can be programmed to keep bothering workers—like the sales bots that keep texting you after you make the mistake of giving a retailer your number—if they don't fill out a time sheet or complete some critical form or orientation. The same tactics that have been programmed into customer relations management systems for generating more sales are, perhaps unsurprisingly, also useful for herding deskless workers. And they're not used only for supervision and management; some of the bots that Nyfty.AI makes enable, for example, workers to get a permit on the spot if they need it to do a particular part of their job. On the back end, Nyfty.AI writes all data directly to the system of record it integrates with, which also eliminates all the data entry and related administrative overhead supervisors usually have to deal with. Everything that used to be done on paper and scanned into these systems—time sheets, forms, waivers, inspection reports—is now pushed to the cloud in what is the construction site equivalent of the self-service checkout at the grocery store. This system saves Rogers-O'Brien and its workers thousands of hours a month in total, said Todd.

One of the most interesting things about Nyfty.AI is that, despite resembling AI in how it functions and what it does, it isn't really AI at all, even by the most expansive definition of that term. In order to make its operations transparent to the supervisors and IT people integrating it with construction site systems of record such as Procore and Autodesk Construction Cloud, the bot is actually entirely rules based, instead of using an AI chatbot on the back end. It's just conventional software, the kind of thing any skilled coder could implement given enough time. All of the "AI agents" that can be built with Nyfty.AI are actually just long, scripted decision trees—essentially, flow charts—that guide the different types of workers on a site, from the highest-ranking construction manager to the greenest laborer.

The fact that the rise of AI chatbots is helping a company such as Nyfty.AI gain new customers illustrates an unexpected impact of the rise of this kind of AI: It's conditioning all of us to think of interacting with computers and other digital systems through conversational interfaces as completely normal.

It's easy to think that these kinds of interfaces were the obvious outcome of our near-universal adoption of smartphones and texting, but I can personally attest that this isn't the case. In about 2013, in the early days of one of my first staff jobs as a tech journalist at an outfit called Quartz, our developers created an app that you could chat with in order to get that day's news. It was a fun novelty, but people didn't really take to it, and eventually the team killed it off. Today, tens of millions of people all over the world chat with AIs constantly, and as chatbots have gained access to search capabilities that enable them to connect to the live internet, talking to them about the news of the day has become unremarkable.

The fact that it took this long for people to adopt the habit of consuming news and other information through a chat interface shows just how sticky our habits can be—and also suggests the possibilities that are opening up as we become accustomed to new ways of interacting with computers. For example, while today's AIs now excel at processing speech and responding in naturalistic voices, norms about how we interact with our devices, especially in open-plan offices, mean that talking to our computers the way actors always did in, say, *Star Trek,* have yet to be updated. It seems certain that in time that will change, although it may take a number of other accommodations and new forms of infrastructure to make it happen.

HISTORY BREAK

How Technology Spreads

Many people are familiar with the idea of the "technology adoption life cycle," even if they've never seen a chart of the bell-shaped curve it describes. Anytime someone uses the phrase "early adopter," they're referencing this life cycle. The idea is dead simple: At first only a very small portion of the population, less than 5 percent, adopts a new technology such as the latest kind of AI. Then the early adopters come along; together these two groups represent maybe 15 to 20 percent of the population. Then the bulk of folks get on board, the next 50 to 60 percent or so, in a couple of waves known as the early and late majorities. Last, there are the laggards—the folks who refuse to give up their Filofaxes, penny farthings, landlines, and cable TV boxes.

The tech adoption life cycle is a good enough way to think about technology adoption, in that it describes a blindingly obvious fact: that some people get a kick out of adopting the next new thing as early as possible, whereas most prefer to wait. The technology adoption cycle was first proposed in 1956 in an obscure paper about farmers and their tech adoption habits. In 1991, Geoffrey Moore published a book called *Crossing the Chasm: Marketing and Selling High-Tech Products to Mainstream Customers* that popularized our modern concept of it and added the useful point that many innovations never get over a "chasm" that happens sometime around the early adoption cycle and actually die out before being more widely adopted. Think of eight-track tapes, laser discs, minidiscs, the Io-mega Zip Drive, and, well, pretty much every dead media format of the past half century.

That litany of bygone formats illustrates one of the key weaknesses of framing everything in terms of the technology adoption life cycle, which is that it really describes only the fate of individual technologies, not whole industries. For that, you need something bigger and more Schumpeterian. (For those unfamiliar with the term, Joseph Schumpeter was the economist who came up with the notion of "creative destruction.")

That's where the history of technological revolutions comes in. Carlota Perez is a Venezuelan British scholar who published a seminal book on the subject, *Technological Revolutions and Financial Capital*, in 2002. It's brilliant and deserves to be every bit as well known as other ideas about the progress of technology, such as Clayton Christensen's notion of disruption and the "innovator's dilemma."

Briefly, what Perez researched and wrote about in a rigorous way was not only the past five biggest technological revolutions but their economic consequences. She boiled down the technology adoption cycle to its two most important periods. the initial time of development of a technology and its adoption by the few, followed by its spread and adoption by the masses. In her study, she described two important corollaries of these two phases of tech adoption.

The first is that the factor that enables mass adoption of a technology—but also slows the rate at which it's adopted—is that a great deal of infrastructure and other technologies must be built to enable and support its mass adoption.

An easy-to-understand example of this is the age of steam and railways, which kicked off in 1829 in Great Britain and made the British Empire possible. While that age came about because of the invention and refinement of the steam engine, the infrastructure that both spread the invention and gave it significant impact included rails for steam-powered trains as well as ports for handing off the goods the trains transported.

Dr. Perez's framework captures just how widespread and far reaching are the consequences of the adoption of a new general-purpose technology such as AI. And her analysis suggests something important and counterintuitive for its future: The bigger its eventual impact, the slower its widespread adoption may be. That's because so much other infrastructure must be built and so many other systems and ways of working must be changed for its consequences to play out.

The other important thing her work uncovered was that in the inflection point between early and widespread adoption, there is typically a financial bubble during what she called the "frenzy period," as huge amounts of cash are poured into the building of the new technology and the infrastructure to support it. Anyone considering the hundreds of billions of dollars currently being poured into AI data centers can't help but raise an eyebrow at a level of investment reminiscent of the money poured into building the infrastructure of the internet around the time of the dot-com bubble of 1999–2000.

The frenzy period is often followed by an economic crash and social upheaval. This isn't just a consequence of overinvestment; it's also a product of the way a new general-purpose technology generates outsize returns—monetary, political, and otherwise—for its early adopters and leads to economic and other inequalities.

It is possible that, decades hence, we'll all look at the dawn of AI as the beginning of the next big industrial and technological revolution after the previous boom created by computers and the internet. If that's the case, the downside is that we may be entering an age that will lead to upheaval, economic and otherwise, as a direct consequence of both investment in and the effectiveness of AI.

If workers are significantly more productive when they can talk to their computers rather than typing at them, will it mean the end of the open-plan office? Will those soundproof phone booths at work that are never available when you need one multiply until there's one for every deskbound worker, turning our workspaces into endless rows of enclosed pods? Or will something like Shiftall's Mutalk, a microphone enclosure that fits over your entire mouth and is held on to your head with a strap, which one YouTuber memorably called a "muzzle for gamers," become a standard-issue part of every office worker's gear? All of this sounds absurd, but it's no stranger than our current mode of deskbound computer work would have appeared to a guild worker of the Middle Ages. It illustrates what Carlota Perez emphasizes about technological revolutions: that much of their impact and a primary reason they take so long to play out is that to make the most of a new technology, so much infrastructure has to be built and so many norms have to change.

"My thing that I always say is 'Forms are dead,'" said Kris Lengieza, a vice president at Procore. The way work is done on construction sites is that people have conversations about it, so making conversational interfaces the dominant way that everyone completes documentation is natural for that environment, he added.

One example is the two most dreaded and time-consuming pieces of documentation on a work site: the request for information and the request for change. Teams on construction sites use Slack and Microsoft Teams just like everyone else in the world of work, but now they're able to automate the production of forms within them when someone in the chat flags the fact that they might need to produce one of these documents to clarify some point about the project they're working on, or ask for permission to change the plans because, for example, it becomes clear that putting an electrical panel into a particular place just won't work. "Let's say that you're having a conversation in Microsoft Teams about something with your team, and you're like 'We got to get a resolution to this,'" said Kris. "You can now invoke the RFI agent to go and create that RFI based on that conversation and fill all the information in for you so that you don't actually have to go do it yourself."

These kinds of agents reduce a process that previously took minutes to seconds, and, given the exigencies of working on a job site, the AI probably writes a better and clearer RFI. The system leverages the large language models that Procore is already tapping into and adds context from the existing project to the prompt. In its operation, an RFI-writing AI agent is remarkably similar to the freelance job–applying AI agent made by PouncerAI discussed in chapter 3. Both are narrowly focused pieces of software that surround an AI with as much scaffolding as possible while giving it the context it needs to generate a communication that a human can quickly review and sign off on. This kind of knowledge work, which sits at the intersection of tedious, annoying, and easy for generative AI to handle, is by far the best kind of task to hand off. (Recall the Eighth Law of AI: Give it your least favorite things to do.)

One consequence of AI helping humans speed through the kind of toil that time sheets, forms, document reviews, takeoffs, and the other necessary but cumbersome paperwork discussed above is that some of this kind of work might actually increase in volume. The consumption of more of a good once it's made cheap, either economically or in terms of some other precious resource, such as time, is called the Jevons Paradox. It's something that heads of AI companies and divisions cite often to explain to analysts and the public why they think that the cheaper and more accessible AI becomes, the more of it will be consumed.

The classic example of the Jevons Paradox is energy. Across all of human history, the cheaper and more accessible it's become, the more of it we gobble up. In 2023, the United States consumed 93.59 quadrillion British Thermal Units (BTUs) of energy—most of it oil, some of it natural gas, the rest coal, renewables, and nuclear—a number so large that it sounds made up. That works out to nearly 280 million BTUs for every U.S. resident, or the equivalent of 2,240 gallons of gasoline for each of us. People who lived in the Middle Ages consumed about a tenth as much energy per day as the average American now does, and that's just individual energy consumption and doesn't include the vast quantities of energy used by manufacturing, data centers, and the like.

Over the years, I've spoken with Aaron Levie, the CEO of Box, many times about the way he sees people across the tech industry turning to AI as a kind of robot in a factory that can help automate simple tasks. In one of our conversations, he asked, "What happens if intelligence is just literally infinitely available and basically free? What will that mean to software in the future?"

Here's what he wrote when answering that question later:

> The biggest opportunities in AI will not be just doing what we already do in software at a lower cost, but instead solving problems that the customer previously didn't solve because it was too expensive or inefficient to go after before.
>
> The far bigger markets will be bringing automation and intelligence to the use-cases that never had them before. The ideal markets will generally be categories where *some* companies could afford to automate or solve the problem in some pockets, but doing so at scale has generally been too expensive or complicated for most customers to tackle.
>
> AI lets you bring automation and intelligence to those use-cases for a far wider set of customers.

The Twentieth Law of AI:
When successfully implemented,
AI scales up rote knowledge work.

Steve Jobs once said that computers are like a "bicycle for our minds," explaining that humans aren't the fastest runners, but that on such a device, we can beat any other creature. I can think of no better metaphor for today's AI, even agentic AI; it's a bicycle for our minds. Importantly, a bicycle is not a thing we imagine has agency or any capabilities of its own.

AI agents in construction illustrate this principle. No matter how much historical data a company accumulates, no matter how many ways it ties together various pieces of software automation and AI—from automatic takeoffs to predictions of delays and cost overruns—these agents can't replace people, only augment them and enable them to move faster. "Obviously, at the end of the day, you still have to have a human in the loop, because none of these agents are perfect, and construction especially is so complex, and the drawings are so complex, and so many trades have to overlay the same ones," said Rajitha at Procore.

This might seem to contradict the nature of some of the agents—such as customer service agents—that I described in chapter 5. But even these agents have a human in the loop, in the sense that a person can be routed to a human when their question is not answered by an AI. And while it might seem as though it's only a matter of time before today's generative AI-powered AI agents take on superhuman powers and become something like digital employees that companies hire instead of humans, there is every indication that the fundamental limitations of the current approaches to AI will stymie those efforts.

Take, for example, the vogue for reasoning models in AI. While these can be helpful in certain domains with easily identifiable goals—a black-and-white right-or-wrong answer, as in coding and mathematics—research has made it apparent that these models are actually *worse* in ways that are critical to how most everyday people would want to use them. Specifically, more recent and more powerful reasoning models hallucinate—that is, lie confidently—much more than previous models did, and it appears that the reason they do is that the particular method of training them, called "reinforcement learning," causes them to hallucinate more often.

Reinforcement learning is why reasoning models are so much better at tasks such as solving complicated math or coding problems, so it appears that there is an unavoidable trade-off between STEM-based reasoning ability and the confident spouting of nonsense in fields about which a model isn't as much of an expert. (I'll leave the uncomfortable parallels between the tendencies of AI reasoning models and their human equivalents to the imagination of the reader.)

Yann LeCun at Meta has declared that this inherent challenge of reasoning models—the longer they reason, the more their inherent tendency to hallucinate compounds, leading them to incorrect answers—is why they are "doomed" as a path to more humanlike intelligence. In the near term, mounting evidence of their limitations suggests that despite some companies' claims, they cannot be the engines of future autonomous AI agents. AI agents powered by reasoning models are, in short, mathematically destined to run amok, messing up internal systems, ordering too much printer paper, confidently giving wrong answers to customers, and committing who knows what other kinds of mischief. One study even found that better reasoning models had a probably ineradicable tendency to try to *escape the confines of their directives* and behave maliciously when given access to outside tools.

America's chief information officers are all too aware of the unreliability of AI agents and the risks that come with their making mistakes. At a *Wall Street Journal* event in Menlo Park, California, in early 2025, one of my colleagues polled the CIOs in attendance and found that while more than 60 percent were experimenting with AI agents in their businesses, their number one concern was their lack of reliability. Those who sell AI agents, in an attempt to generate fear of missing out—or the modern, AI-age equivalent, fear of falling behind—are insistent that businesses that don't adopt them quickly enough will become dinosaurs. And while that may be true in some cases, what it leaves out is that figuring out how humans can review the work of AI agents or be prompted to give input as they operate may prove to be the biggest and most challenging problem of implementing them.

If you've made it this far, I encourage you to send me an email—subject line: Loyal Reader—with your thoughts on the book. I promise to write back. (Life hack: Every *Wall Street Journal* reporter's email address is right there on our individual "about" pages.) You should also take a moment to feel proud of yourself for making it through what I realize has been, despite my best efforts, some occasionally dense and challenging material. You've now attained a level of understanding of the state of today's AI that, I hope, gives you the confidence to explore how you can use it in your own work and life. If after a stretch break and another beverage you're ready to level up to an understanding of how to think about the future of AI, the third and final section of this book is for you.

TERMS

Deskless workers: Almost four in ten workers in the United States do not work at a desk. AI promises to have as profound an impact on the way these workers do their jobs as mobile devices did.

Technology adoption life cycle: A model of how tech is adopted, starting with a small number of innovators, followed by a larger number of early adopters and then the majority of people. During the early adoption phase, many technologies die out and fail to cross the chasm of adoption by a mainstream audience.

Technological revolutions: The big-brained version of the technology adoption life cycle is known as the Carlota Perez framework, or the theory of technological revolutions. Rather than looking at a single invention, her work studies the collections of technology that transform the world and lead to financial manias, followed by widespread adoption of not just new technologies but the infrastructure that enables them. A classic example is the way the steam engine led to the steam train, which could transform the world only once the world was crisscrossed with railroad tracks. It's at least plausible that AI is leading to a similar economic transformation, although it may be merely part of a larger, longer-running cluster of changes brought about by the PC and the internet, making it not a revolution in itself but a form of infrastructure that enables a much broader one.

Rules-based system: Conventional software in which every part is explicitly coded by a human being is rules based, in contrast to an AI system, which learns a set of behaviors. Rules-based systems that present as what we've come to know as AIs—for example, through a chatbot—are seeing an uptick in adoption as AI makes us all more familiar with this mode of interaction.

Jevons Paradox: The postulate, often borne out in historical studies, that when something becomes cheaper and more abundant, people will use more of it, erasing any gains created by increased efficiency in the production of that good or service. Energy is the classic example—people will use as much of it as they can afford—but it's now being applied to AI, as the cost per token for AI models rapidly falls.

Reinforcement learning: A process in machine learning and AI in which behaviors that yield a correct answer are reinforced (or "rewarded"), while those that do not are extinguished. A concept originally borrowed from studies of animal behavior, reinforcement learning does not require a deep learning system in order to be implemented. Its most famous applications are in AIs used to play games, specifically the AlphaGo system, which beat the human world champion in the game of Go. One form of reinforcement learning, which aligns the outputs of large language models with human preferences by having humans evaluate its output, has been key to creating chatbots that people find useful and enjoy interacting with. Another form is key to training reasoning models to become better at tasks with easily identifiable correct and incorrect answers, such as math and coding.

SUMMARY

What to Know

AI agents work best when they're treated like robots in factories tasked with discrete tasks, rather than as autonomous workers with a broader remit. There is an inverse relationship between how autonomous they can be and how much they can accomplish in a fully automated way. There are many unexpected applications for AI agents that are well outside what their deskbound creators are currently focused on, especially for the nearly four in ten workers in the

United States (and something like seven in ten workers globally) who don't sit at a desk all day.

How to Think About It

Chatbots and eventually voice-based interfaces are the results of human-centered design that once animated the revolution in user interfaces that Apple popularized. Generative AI is particularly good at making information accessible in this way. The most successful AI agents will be amalgamations of other AIs, some of them classical and based on large proprietary data sets, others rules-based systems that under the hood aren't AI at all.

What Questions to Ask

How tailored to my industry is the particular AI agent I'm being sold? How can I measure the ways in which it will—or won't—speed up my existing workflows? What other measures of success do I value, aside from productivity? What other dependencies and commitments—financial and otherwise—are required to get the most out of this AI agent? How much lock-in to a particular vendor am I committing to by adopting this agent, and what options, if any, do I have for using alternate systems as they arise?

Part III

SO YOU WANT TO BUILD
YOUR OWN AI

11

WE, ROBOT

On January 7, 2025, a day when his firm could boast that it was the most valuable company on earth, NVIDIA CEO Jensen Huang stood on a giant stage in Las Vegas before an audience of six thousand tech enthusiasts, feeling himself. In a shiny black alligator leather version of his trademark jacket, he began his keynote speech at that year's Consumer Electronics Show by roaring "DO YOU LIKE MY JACKET?"

The audience roared back. The man whom some people call "AI Jesus" was in his element, holding court in front of a sold-out, cavernous auditorium full of adoring business casual–clad geeks, plus tens of thousands more who were live streaming his speech all over the world. NVIDIA's stock price had never been higher. Jensen was personally worth more than $100 billion, one of the ten wealthiest people on the planet. It was, to that point, the pinnacle of NVIDIA's—and Jensen's—power, influence, and cultural cachet. Everyone wanted either to be with NVIDIA through some kind of partnership or to become NVIDIA, leading to endless fawning profiles of the company's unique corporate structure.

And it was all due to AI. In the new gold rush to create what every other tech company and white-hot startup had declared was the biggest thing since humanity tamed fire, NVIDIA was the pick and shovel dealer. If AI was the next industrial revolution,

NVIDIA was providing the steam engines *and* the rails for them to run on. The moment invited comparison to the peak of the dot-com era in 1999—a time that many of those powering this new revolution were too young to remember.

Onstage, Jensen didn't want to revisit his company's recent triumphs or even dwell too long on the coming leaps in power for the microchips and "AI supercomputers" his company builds. A man known for speaking extemporaneously every time he appears in public—making his every declaration a direct expression of his current obsessions—was instead laser focused on what he wanted to convince the audience would be the next big chapter in the world-altering saga of AI: robotics.

Standing in front of a stage-spanning projector screen filled with life-size images of humanoid robots from well-funded startups including Boston Dynamics, Agility Robotics, and Figure, he declared that "The ChatGPT moment for general robotics is just around the corner."

Thousands of miles away—in Sunnyvale and Austin, Hangzhou and Boston, Brooklyn and Salem, Oregon—Figure, Apptronik, Unitree Robotics, Boston Dynamics, Reflex Robotics, and Agility Robotics, respectively, were jockeying to be the lead contender to build the robot body that AI running on Jensen's microchips would animate, like God breathing life into Adam. Meanwhile, at Google DeepMind in London and the Jeff Bezos– and OpenAI-backed Physical Intelligence in San Francisco, others were working on that AI.

All of these efforts lie at the cutting edge of AI development, but that's not why they're relevant to those of us trying to use AI in our everyday lives. The reason they matter is that the application of AI in the physical world—a phenomenon called "embodied intelligence"—is redefining AI.

Moving AI into the physical world creates a feedback loop that has the potential to solve the limitations of how much data is available to train today's AIs. The more autonomous vehicles, drones, robots, and sensors we put into the world, the more opportunities they have to observe and gather information of every kind. This new font of data is already being fed back into existing systems, giving them new abilities to recognize and act on visual and auditory data. It's also going to make it possible for computers to start showing up in our lives in new ways in the form of augmented reality (think of smart glasses) and robotics (think of robots finally becoming commonplace in public spaces, our roads and skies, and our homes).

Having built up an understanding of the inner workings, capabilities, and limitations of today's easily accessible AIs, we can now turn to where AI is going and how it's going to have a profound impact on how we interact with the digital world.

A CHATGPT MOMENT FOR ROBOTICS?

Over the months leading up to Jensen's announcement, in conversations with engineers and CEOs at many companies, it had become clear to me that robots were nowhere near a "ChatGPT moment"—that is, a technological breakthrough that would rapidly lead to a humanlike and broadly usable system that would quickly usher robots into all our lives. But that didn't mean we weren't at a critical juncture for robotics as a whole or that Jensen's instincts were wrong. An unusually technical CEO even among leaders of tech companies, he was, after all, seeing the rapid evolution of AI for robotics from the inside. He knew that the same AI driving most of the systems mentioned in this book— the transformer architecture invented at Google in the mid-2010s, which made ChatGPT possible—was also enabling entirely new ways of creating robot "brains."

Taking a system that had proved capable of simulating intelligence by blabbering at easily fooled humans and forcing it to inhabit and operate a physical body was already definitively illustrating just how far this kind of AI had to go before it could approach the intelligence of a cockroach, much less a person. Or, as Yann LeCun told me when we visited one afternoon in a small conference room of the New York City outpost of Meta, the one secreted behind glass doors at the back of the expansive, light-filled Moynihan Train Hall, AI isn't even as intelligent as a cat.

Despite their size and complexity, at the most basic level, large language models are next-word predictors. "And the basic flaw with this is that contrary to humans and animals, there is no understanding of the physical world, so no common sense," LeCun said as he warmed to a subject he had addressed in talks many times before. "It has no real sort of intuition or really a sense of how the world works, right? And there's a lot of people doing experiments to show that, indeed, those systems don't really understand the nature of the world."

Looking professorial in his black-framed eyeglasses and artfully rumpled button-down, he continued in the Parisian accent and playful-but-stern tone that he uses to command whatever discussion he's a part of. "The second thing is, they don't really have persistent memory in the sense of being able to retrieve some information other than by painful learning. You have to augment them with something called RAG." RAG, which stands for retrieval-augmented generation, basically means searching a body of documents using either conventional keyword search or semantic search, and adding the contents of the documents referenced or relevant passages thereof to the context window of an AI. It's a system that can work well for using AI to generate answers from a knowledge base, as in being applied to customer service at a textbook company, sharing knowledge in a construction company, or using an AI to help organize a large project in something such as NotebookLM. But as a kind of memory, it's a hack, since unlike the memory of an animal, it doesn't represent a fundamental rewiring of the neural network that comprises the AI.

"When you think about something, you sort of manipulate some sort of mental model of what you're thinking of or what you're planning to do," LeCun continued. "AIs don't do this. And then the last two things that they're incapable of doing, really, is reasoning and planning. And this is something that, you know, animals like cats are absolutely capable of."

It's these four things—understanding the physical world, having persistent memory, and being able to reason and plan—that today's AIs cannot do. It's the mission of Meta's FAIR division, which LeCun heads, to come up with a fundamentally new and different architecture for AI—a system that, in its finest details, will operate quite differently from today's transformer-based AI systems. The goal is to create a system that can someday do all of the things a human—or a cat—can do; the very things required to make autonomous, or at least much more capable, robots a reality.

Yann and Meta have plenty of competition. Just two months after we spoke, Physical Intelligence, a company based in San Francisco, announced that it had raised $400 million to realize its own version of Yann's dream. "We want to build a model that can control any robot to do any task, including all the robots that exist today and robots that haven't even been developed yet," Karol Hausman, a cofounder and the CEO of Physical Intelligence, told me at the time.

Just two months after that, in January 2025, Elon Musk said that Tesla would build ten thousand AI-powered humanoid robots by the end of that year. (Later, no one was surprised when the company failed to do so, given Musk's long history of delayed or indefinitely postponed delivery of his promises. He once admitted in an interview that he is excessively optimistic about timelines for delivering his promises—but many analysts have observed this is key to pushing his employees to deliver on what could otherwise be unrealistic goals.)

In February 2025, the Sunnyvale-based Figure was reportedly

in talks to be valued at $40 billion, and by March, Alphabet's DeepMind subsidiary—the company started by Demis Hassabis and then acquired in 2014 by Google—announced a pair of AI models intended to be the brains of robots, starting with the Austin-based Apptronik's humanoid robots.

More versatile AI, such as the kind built by DeepMind, was "the last piece of the puzzle" required to make Apptronik's robots useful and commercially viable, said Apptronik CEO Jeff Cardenas. He had spent nine years building Apptronik, which had originally been spun out of a robotics lab at the University of Texas at Austin. Most of that time, the company had bootstrapped itself on military contracts and had sought venture capital only once he was confident that his team had cracked the problem of how to build an affordable robot body. (That turned out to be mostly about figuring out how to cheaply manufacture the specialized motors, gearboxes, and sensors, collectively called actuators, that are the "muscles" of such a body.) "The idea was, if we're building the best robots in the world, that will allow us to attract the best AI teams in the world," he said. "And then, you know, generative AI came along."

Generative AI is a unique enabler of Cardenas's robot brains for two reasons. The first is the transformer architecture itself, which has proved to be more capable than deep learning on its own. The second is that the systems being built with transformer models—the attempts to nudge us closer to some kind of artificial general intelligence, however incremental—are themselves useful for beginning to give robots a sense of the real world.

FROM LARGE LANGUAGE MODELS TO VISION-LANGUAGE-ACTION MODELS

The future of robotics is important for the future of the kinds of AIs discussed throughout this book, because solving the problems of making AIs function in the real world—making them animate a physical body—requires making them better at understanding our world. It seems likely, at this point, that in the same way attempting to go to the moon led to all sorts of new scientific and technical breakthroughs in related realms, setting ourselves this task will mean creating AIs that do things that are impossible for the current generation of them. This transition from what are effectively AI brains in a jar to embodied intelligence is something long anticipated by researchers in the field, especially those familiar with the ways in which biological intelligences develop throughout adolescence.

We have to start with how large language models—the things powering ChatGPT since its debut—are becoming what are known as vision-language models. Put simply, companies building frontier AIs, including Google DeepMind, OpenAI, Meta, Amazon, and others began to mix more and more images into the training data they fed their large language models (LLMs). On a slightly deeper level—and yes, we are getting a tiny bit technical here—the way these models are trained is that images and video are encoded by an algorithm invented at OpenAI and revealed in early 2021, called Contrastive Language-Image Pre-training (CLIP). This algorithm turns images and video into the same kinds of vectors that encode words in an LLM, allowing them to be associated with text just as other words would be. By rendering visual data into an abstraction that can be handled by a transformer, OpenAI's engineers had figured out a way to bridge the world of computer vision algorithms and LLMs. Alongside the rise of reinforcement learning–powered reasoning models, it's fair to say that vision-language models were the next sizable breakthrough after transformer architecture.

Now that we have some sense of what a vision-language model is, it's possible to talk about the thing that comes after that: a vision-language-action (VLA) model, which is, its creators claim, the true do-it-all multihyphenate of the robotics world, able to see, understand, *and* act, all of its systems driven by a single integrated system. The evolution of these models has been short but rapid—from the first transformer-powered robot model in early 2022 to a truly integrated VLA in 2025, in models from Google called Gemini Robotics and Figure in the form of Helix. What's key here is that just as vision-language models are trained through a method that integrates both images and words, vision-language-action models add robot actions to the mix.

The whole thing is a massive bet on the idea that transformer models are, if not the end-all, then the be-all models that can function enough like a living brain to yield a system that can function with the versatility that general-purpose robots—think everything from factory workers to robot butlers—will require.

There are a number of monumental challenges to be overcome in order to realize that dream. And given the inherent limitations of transformers described throughout this book, there's reason to believe that it will take a fundamentally different architecture to get us there. Just to get us to square one on this journey—a robot that can do the most basic of tasks, such as grabbing a drink from the fridge or picking up a piece of trash and throwing it away—will require massive amounts of data that don't currently exist.

To date, all of the huge breakthroughs in the apparent abilities of AI have been due to the fact that there is an internet's worth of data out there free—for now, anyway—for the taking by tech companies. (The legality of scraping all that data is in question, and while advocates for using it claim that it's no different from a human learning from the internet, I hope that by now it's apparent why that's a facile comparison and why figuring out some way to compensate creators of the data on which generative AI depends would be, at the least, the fair thing to do.) This goes for large language models, video and image generators, even specialized systems that are intended for specific fields, such as medicine or the law.

"The first models we've been building with these AIs are based on the data that's readily available to us," said Rev Lebaredian, a vice president at NVIDIA who sits atop the interlocking parts of the organization-building systems necessary to train robots. "It was information on the internet, most of which is just language, just text, and is the easiest kind of data to find. If you combine mountains of data and enormous supercomputing capabilities, out comes this neural network that seems to understand language completely. The idea is that if you can also give it data about the world—physics, the state of the world, how things behave—the same way, it can figure out all the patterns for language, it can figure out all the rules of the physical world."

An obvious flaw in this reasoning is that while language is a relatively constrained system full of formal rules and a finite vocabulary, the real, physical world is unbounded in too many ways to name. To imagine that today's AIs could cope with such a world is to subscribe to the belief that they are capable of building actual world models, the way a human or even most animals do. But if the experts who believe that transformer-based models are more like bags of heuristics are correct, the amount of data and computations it will take to make robots functional in the real world may so far exceed what today's systems are capable of that the project is basically a nonstarter. What's more, even if we could come up with the resources to both train these systems and run them on robots, the inherently brittle nature of their AIs would make them unusable.

These realities aren't stopping those determined to build AI brains for robots, however, nor should they, because there's still a path to creating more flexible robots that will be usable in the real world. The recipe, as ever, is to ask less of these robots and put them into controlled environments, such as warehouses and factories. The answer, in other words, is the real-world equivalent of the software scaffolding that already makes so many other AIs useful.

Agility Robotics' rollout in a Spanx warehouse in an exurb of Atlanta, Georgia, is a good example of this phenomenon. Melonee Wise, a veteran of the robotics industry who is now chief technology officer at Agility, corrects me when I ask her about the trial of Agility's two-legged, crate-carrying robot Digit at the warehouse. "It's not a trial, it's deployed," she said—making it the first commercial deployment of a humanoid robot anywhere in the world. So far, Digit's role is limited: In a cordoned-off area, it marches to low, wheeled, ground-hugging robots that roll up with plastic totes full of goods on their flat tops, grabs the totes, then trundles them over to a conveyor belt.

Beginning in the summer of 2023, "We focused on delivering not just a robot but an enterprise solution," she added. "We have a cloud platform, a third-party support system that does tier one and two support, and end-to-end workflows that enable our customers to tackle more than just one activity. It's real-world, real-life stuff, like stacking, destacking, palletizing, depalletizing, AMRs, shelving, and flow racks."

Translated from logistics speak, that means that Agility is now providing a system that operates on its own, is maintained by a third party to maximize its uptime, and can do many of the most tedious but necessary tasks required in an e-commerce fulfillment warehouse. Systems to automate the flow of goods through this kind of building come in dozens of different flavors, many of them custom combinations of bits of automation offered by a variety of companies. (There is a whole book on this subject—see my previous one, *Arriving Today: From Factory to Front Door—Why Everything Has Changed About How and What We Buy*—if you're curious.)

What makes Agility's robots different—and what every company trying to build some part of the AI-driven robot stack is betting on—is that robots powered by modern AI are more flexible than current forms of automation. Being roughly human

shaped, they can move about in spaces designed for us and operate in places where space is at a premium. They can also switch
tasks throughout a day, a critical form of flexibility that humans
possess and that, to date, no robotic system has. Warehouses typically go through cycles of ingesting, sorting, and disgorging
goods, and humans—or humanlike robots—need to be able to
take on a variety of jobs throughout a day, week, or season.

ANOTHER MOUNTAIN TO CLIMB

Robots aren't just the next big thing in AI because bringing AI to
physical labor is the next opportunity to make money with the
technology; they're also the next big thing in AI because there is a
growing belief that without systems such as robots that gather
data in the real world, AI may stall in its tracks for lack of data to
train on.

In late 2024, Ilya Sutskever, a cofounder of OpenAI who had
left the summer before to found his own AI company, said what
many people had already been thinking: Companies building
cutting-edge AI had run out of data to train on. They had vacu-
umed up the entire open internet for their large language models.
It was an admission that many of their abilities were about data
rather than raw computing power. The reason he'd gone ahead
and founded his own AI startup was that he'd found "a different
mountain to climb." Presumably, he'd had an intuition about a
totally different way to achieve machine intelligence.

In the meantime, every other big AI lab wasn't going to
wait. And at the intersection of robots and seemingly unrelated
technologies—augmented reality, the metaverse, digital twins—
was an opportunity to keep climbing using the tools already at
hand. But doing so was going to require a three-pronged approach
to creating—or mining—new sources of data.

Karol Hausman spent almost six years as a research scientist at
Google Brain in Mountain View, California, which was Google's

AI division before the company combined it with the other AI company it owned, DeepMind, to form Google DeepMind. During the second half of his tenure there, he worked on robotics until 2004, when he left to form Physical Intelligence. That puts him into direct competition with his former colleagues, the ones building the AI brain for Apptronik's—and others'—robots.

The state of the art in training robots is to have humans teleoperate them and use their actions as training data. This approach is a direct analog to how previous AIs were trained on human-generated content. The difference is that since we don't have an internet's worth of this kind of data, companies have to create their own.

To that end, Google DeepMind has partnered with Stanford Robotics Center to create the Mobile ALOHA system, which has to be seen to be believed. Picture a room full of desks, something like a large public school classroom. At every desk, there is a pair of manipulators controlled by a human and a pair of arms with hands that the humans can operate using their manipulators. Now imagine people seated at all of those dozens of desks, using the manipulators to direct the robot hands to do every kind of mundane task imaginable, from folding socks to throwing away a piece of trash. One demo from the paper on the second generation of this system even shows a person using the robot hands to open a disposable contact lens container and put the lens onto a toy dog, raising the specter of a future in which we're going to allow robots to perform the most intimate and delicate of tasks on our bodies.

Karol's approach at Physical Intelligence is similar. The company's big coming-out product was a robot that can climb what turns out to be the Mount Everest of robot challenges: folding laundry. "The reason laundry is particularly interesting is it turns out you can't really script it, because any piece of clothing can be in so many different configurations," he said. "We as programmers can't prescribe how to fold clothes. This is why it's been a long-standing challenge for robots."

A lot of robotics research involves trying to figure out how to get robots to accomplish complicated tasks without their having to be shown every possible movement required to do so. Karol compares what he and his team are working on to a sort of large language model but for robot actions, which should allow a robot to handle situations it hasn't seen before.

"Something that was very eye opening is that you can start from a pretrained VLM like GPT-4," he said. "So it has some of that world knowledge already encoded, and you can repurpose it for robots, and some of that knowledge translates to robot behavior. Before, it was thought you'd have to demonstrate every possible action and object for a robot, which was not possible to do. Now they can get that basic understanding of the world from VLMs, and they understand certain concepts without being exposed to them."

But we're not very far down this path yet. When I asked him whether his robot could come into my house and fold the mountain of laundry that my brood is constantly generating, he said that for now, every time the robot is in a new environment, it requires a great deal of additional training to allow it to cope. "If I brought a robot like that in our video to your home, it's not going to work. It requires a bit of data in your environment: your folding table, your house. The model does not generalize yet." It's also slow and it sometimes fails, even under the best of circumstances. "As proud as we are of our accomplishment and the model we showed, we are still at the beginning," he added.

The experiences of an ex-Google, Stanford-trained AI expert building a robotics company focused on someday displacing all manual labor might not seem like it has much relevance to the rest of us mere mortals and our workaday applications for AI. But for any business focused on differentiating itself by partnering with others to build its own AI systems, the lesson is clear: Doing so requires sources of data that might not yet exist—or are inaccessible.

A common refrain of the pre–generative AI days, when classic AI required huge amounts of labor by data scientists, was that "data is the new oil." This phrase has, thankfully, fallen out of fashion—data is neither a finite resource nor a fossil fuel—but it did get at something important about data, which was that it was becoming increasingly valuable. It's worth reviving this idea but for our modern era of trade wars and renewable energy: I think data is the new rare earths.

Rare earth elements, such as yttrium, neodymium, and scandium, are essential for the manufacture of modern high-tech devices, primarily because they're needed for high-strength magnets, which go into everything from electric vehicles and wind turbines to fighter jets and Dyson vacuum cleaners. A funny thing about rare earths is that, being ubiquitous in the earth's crust, they aren't actually rare. Nine-tenths of the world's refined rare earths come from China, not because it has a monopoly on the ore from which they're extracted but because that's where almost all the world's refining capacity is.

The Twenty-First Law of AI: Data is the new rare earths.

Like rare earths, data is ubiquitous but controlled by a handful of players, because what makes it valuable is what it turns into after it's been refined. Doing so requires a huge investment and a willingness to suffer certain undesirable externalities. In the case of rare earths, the undesirable externality is pollution, and in the case of data, it can be issues regarding privacy and ownership. In sum, both rare earths and data are precious commodities *after they've been gathered and refined,* the control of which enables unique leverage in the twenty-first century.

SIMULATION VERSUS EXPERIENCE

Training the AIs that will power the next generation of robots might not require nearly as much data from humans as current approaches suggest. The robots of tomorrow, said Rev Lebaredian of NVIDIA, might learn how to operate in the real world by doing what some have compared to dreaming.

"For robotics, we need to develop algorithms we can't write directly ourselves," said Rev. Those algorithms will govern both how robots perceive the world, and how they control their own bodies. "Both of these things require lots and lots of examples, and we can't get these from the real world. They're not available on the internet, and they're too expensive to generate in real life." The solution, he said, is simulation. "If we can model the world accurately enough, then we have an unlimited source of data and examples to train robot brains." The idea of robots dreaming their way to competency might sound far-fetched, but it's already a common tactic for training the autonomous driving systems that are on the road today.

Rev's title gives us a hint about how these systems work. He's vice president of Omniverse and simulation technology at NVIDIA. To create a generation of robots brought up in simulation, three computers are necessary. The first is the one on board the robot; the second is the supercomputer in the cloud used to train its AI; the third, which is unique to robotics, is what he calls the "Omniverse computer," and it's the one running a realistic, three-dimensional simulation of the real world, complete with physics.

Think of it as something like the 3D environments that video games take place in, only as faithful to reality as possible. In such an environment, self-driving cars can practice what to do when a child runs out into a street as many times as necessary, without consequences. In the same way, an Omniverse computer could create a simulation of your house and the AI that might someday power your robot butler could roam around it, learning its environment until its minders are confident that it can navigate on its own.

The need for all three of these computers is naturally great news for NVIDIA and its investors. If bringing robots into every aspect of our lives will require creating ultrafaithful representations of every location and structure they might encounter, AI supercomputers to train on navigating them, and energy-efficient onboard AI supercomputers inside the robots themselves, NVIDIA will be selling more microchips than ever.

The Twenty-Second Law of AI:
Simulation is the next AI frontier.

In a nondescript warehouse in south San Francisco, the brains of Keller Rinaudo Cliffton's autonomous delivery drones are dreaming about taking flight.

"This is the hardware-in-the-loop simulation," he said, gesturing at rack after rack of exposed, microchip-studded PCB boards covered with blinking lights, each plugged into cables that snake away to nearby servers. Every one of these things is, like Neo in the Matrix, immersed in a simulation of the endless variety of conditions it will encounter as it flies from retailers to people's homes, where a brain like it will someday be at the center of a fifty-five-pound, five-rotor fixed-wing aircraft that will deliver everything from burritos to pharmaceuticals.

"Each of these is the brain of an aircraft and all of the avionics of an aircraft," said Keller. "So you can see the flight computer,

the power distribution board, all the antennas, battery, hover motors and hover motor controllers, mixed motor controller, winch
controller over here—and this is the droid brain here." These are
the guts of the Zipline "droid," the company's name for its flying
delivery robot, which is capable of depositing items onto a spot
the size of a dinner plate, owing to precise control of both the
aircraft and the delivery module, which is suspended at the end of
a three-hundred-foot-long cable that it lowers to the ground.

"All of this is connected to a simulator, and you can kind of
think about like it's in Grand Theft Auto, or it's like flying in the
Matrix. They're sort of dreaming, sort of flying in simulation.
This enables us to do a huge amount of testing and validation and
verification of all of their new software, like bug fixes, new features, or performance improvements. We can catch about ninety-
five percent of software errors or problems here, before we then
put them onto real aircraft at the test sites."

Companies often talk about creating a "digital twin" of a complicated system or device, by which they mean a faithful copy of
it that allows for testing. Companies have been creating digital
twins of jet engines and factories, for example, for decades. But
the Omniverse approach—embodied in the real world by systems
such as Zipline's—is in a way the inverse of that strategy. Rather
than simulating an object, it simulates the whole world. This enables builders of robots, be they wheeled, legged, or flying, to
allow their hardware to inhabit that simulation and learn how to
complete tasks safely.

I've saved for the last what will be, for some of you, the most
rewarding chapter in this book. Everything you've learned so far
has equipped you to understand what it means to live in an age
when we can create systems that can usefully ingest and manipulate any kind of data we can get our hands on, in whatever field
we work in or are most passionate about.

TERMS

Retrieval-augmented generation (RAG): A system to bolt a sort of memory onto existing large language models. Users asking questions of such a model have parts of their queries directed to a search engine that surfaces documents that are loaded into the LLM's context window, allowing it to operate on them as it would any other long prompt. A key weakness of RAG systems is the search engine itself. Traditional keyword-based search engines can surface documents that aren't related to a user's query, leading the AI to provide incorrect information, a form of hallucination distinct from the kind that usually befalls AI chatbots. Some RAG systems borrow a technique from LLMs, by doing a semantic search on documents, but this requires that the documents first be turned into word embeddings, which can lead to its own problems.

Humanoids: Robots that resemble people—with two arms and two legs—are often called humanoids. But many robotics engineers believe that this definition should be broader and include anything with two arms, whatever it's attached to, whether a four-legged robot body forming a kind of robot centaur or a set of wheels.

Actuators: A key differentiator for some robotics companies, these are the "muscles" of today's robots. Traditionally, they had to be ultraprecise and very strong, making them very expensive. Less precise actuators that are much cheaper to manufacture and are more efficient may be a key enabler of future robots, just as cheaper electric motors have been for electric vehicles.

Embodied intelligence: The study of how nervous systems, bodies, and the environment interact to create intelligence. A growing understanding of the loops of perception and action in biological nervous systems and of the inextricability of intelligence from the environment that gives rise to it is providing a rich set of new techniques, approaches, and avenues of exploration for those who are beginning to put AIs into robot bodies.

Vision-language model: A variant of a large language model in which, during training, images are turned into vectors that a transformer model can train on. This produces multimodal AIs that can process both images and video along with text.

Vision-language-action (VLA) model: One step beyond vision-language models, VLAs incorporate actions into their transformer models. These actions are often recordings of humans puppeteering robots as they move their limbs to perform actions.

Omniverse computer: A system designed to simulate the real world so that robots can learn how to operate within it before they're set loose in the real world

Simulation: The rise of "digital twins" and numerous ways to capture environments and objects means that AI agents— both robots and purely software-based ones—can now be trained in ways that were previously impossible, for example, through reinforcement learning.

SUMMARY
What to Know
Embodied intelligence is necessitating the rapid development of new variants of large language models, including vision-language models

and vision-language-action models. These systems represent a vast new frontier for the development of AI.

How to Think About It

Every company has access to a unique proprietary trove of data that others don't possess—or could start building one in the course of its regular business. As the appetite for specialized data of every kind, not just unstructured text but also images and video, continues to grow, data is once again becoming a valuable and scarce commodity that it's possible to leverage directly or to license.

What Questions to Ask

As robotics and related physical automation bring AI directly into our factories, warehouses, workspaces, and eventually our offices and homes, the same questions outlined throughout this book apply: What problem does this automation solve, and is it necessarily better than all other (simpler, less expensive) alternatives? What kind of AI is powering this system, and where did its training data come from? In terms of capitalizing on a company's existing reserves of novel and proprietary data, what are they, and what more could be gathered in anticipation of their someday being useful?

12

THE MUSEUM OF ALL IDEAS

> My parents sent me to a British public school, that is, a private
> school. Same one that John Cleese went to. I got Christianity at
> school and Stalinism at home. I think that was a very good
> preparation for being a scientist, because I got used to the idea
> that at least half the people are completely wrong.
>
> —Geoffrey Hinton, *Talking Nets:*
> *An Oral History of Neural Network Research*

It all started in B8; more specifically, in the well eight over and
two down on a plate of ninety-six under a microscope on a lab
bench in a research facility near the New York University campus
in Manhattan. In that well, a drop of solution glowed a faint
green when exposed to ultraviolet light, like a blob of radioactive
ooze in a cheesy science fiction film.

The synthetic protein in well B8 gave off just a fiftieth of the
light of the natural protein it was designed to mimic. That substance, known as a green fluorescent protein, is found in *Aequo-
rea victoria,* the crystal jellyfish that dwells in the Pacific Ocean,
and it's a staple of science labs the world over, prized for its ability
to help researchers visualize processes at the cellular level.

With this promising candidate in hand, a subsequent redesign
of the molecular structure of the protein in well B8 yielded something about as good at glowing as the natural substance that had

inspired it. And in that way the researchers who had created it showed that their process for creating new molecules could be applied again and again in search of all kinds of novel and useful substances, from new medicines to never-before-seen enzymes for industry.

The protein in question had been designed not by humans but by an AI. The result was something truly alien, a gigantic molecule so far removed from all of evolution's attempts at creating something like it as to be unheard of in the scientific literature. The scientists involved calculated that it would take 500 million years of natural evolution to create such a molecule. But AI had done it in hours.

The AI was of a unique but by now familiar type: a transformer. But it had not been trained on all the text on the internet, like ChatGPT, or every image and video engineers could get their hands on, like an image generator, or countless hours of human movement or driving, like the control system for a robot or autonomous vehicle; it had been trained on all available scientific literature on the sequence, structure, and function of proteins.

Proteins are the stuff of life. They are the structural and functional parts of every living thing on Earth; they are what DNA is turned into, what enzymes are made of, the machinery of the class of matter we call animate. The company that made that particular AI, EvolutionaryScale, fed the system every scrap of data available on the sequence of amino acids that make up a protein—that is, its code. And also its structure, its particular three-dimensional shape; and, with that structure, what it ultimately does: its function.

In the same way that a visual language model can operate across both text and images, this EvolutionaryScale Model (ESM) can operate on the associations among a protein's sequence, structure, and function. The resulting model is, on some level, something like a simulator of biology itself.

"I think the incredible thing about these methods, which is common across artificial intelligence, is that somehow, from solving this very simple task of predicting the next token, the models capture the underlying information structure of the data, and they can do this better in many cases than models that we try to build from first principles," said Alexander Rives, a cofounder and the chief scientist of EvolutionaryScale. "It's learning to predict the tokens that evolution chooses, so that can be thought of as simulating evolution."

It's an extravagant claim, that a transformer model has divined the hidden relationships between the way the building blocks of life are put together and what they do. It implies that EvolutionaryScale's model has somehow learned basic truths about the most fundamental processes of how the molecular machinery of life changes and adapts over time in response to evolutionary pressure.

Yet Alexander's claim should not be dismissed out of hand, even knowing what we do about the "bag of heuristics" nature of the way that transformer models extract and store information. This AI doesn't have to think and it doesn't have to reason to be able to fluently generate new ideas for proteins, just as a large language model can endlessly disgorge prose. Unlike writing, thinking up new proteins isn't something that billions of humans can already do. So even if this model is a primitive one, it still has the potential to be useful. "Much of AI is being applied to problems where humans are already competent," said Rives. "But the sequences of proteins are unintelligible to the unaided human intellect, and so AI can make this comprehensible."

So far, scientists have used earlier versions of this system to improve antibodies to particular pathogens, including Ebola and SARS-CoV-2; to create a universal atlas of all cell types that could be transformative for basic research; and to predict what a newly discovered enzyme will do, based solely on its sequence.

The potential of AI, like that of EvolutionaryScale, trained on the whole of the scientific literature on organic molecules—treatments for previously incurable diseases, novel materials with properties we can hardly imagine—is big enough on its own. But the broader implications of the applications of transformers to every kind of structured data we can get our hands on is truly mind-boggling. We live at the dawn of an age of generative pre-trained transformers (GPTs) for every field in which data can be gathered and in which there is a discernible structure within that data. ChatGPT may be the granddaddy of them all, but what's coming are new kinds of AI for every field of human endeavor.

For example, transformers are already a part of the models used for short- and long-term weather prediction. The result is forecasts that are both more accurate and stretch farther into the future. They also show promise for stock market prediction, financial analysis, and any other kind of analysis of data that unspools over time. Many of the tasks at which they already excel—translation, speech recognition and generation, image recognition and classification—are only just beginning to make their way into consumer gadgets. As they do, they will have subtle but far-reaching effects on how we interact with the world.

The kind of AI that EvolutionaryScale specializes in has moved the leaders of frontier AI labs to wax hyperbolic in their usual fashion. Dario Amodei, a cofounder and the CEO of Anthropic, has speculated that the eradication of cancer might be at hand; Demis Hassabis of DeepMind has expressed optimism that while we're at it, we might eliminate all communicable diseases. And while this technology shows promise in shaving years off what can be a multidecade development process for new treatments, the wildest of these fantasies, such as the impending debut of super-human machine intelligence, is definitely not in the cards.

However powerful it may prove to be in identifying promising new molecules, the fundamental limiting factor of Evolutionary-

Scale and related AIs—drug companies are now building their own versions—is that while it can narrow the field of candidate substances, they must still run the usual gauntlet of tests in the lab. To create the novel green fluorescent protein, for example, EvolutionaryScale's team had to ask the AI to generate ninety-six different candidates. Then they had to synthesize them all and test each one. Because they were simply trying to see which glowed when exposed to UV light, that was a relatively simple test. The researchers were able to take the promising molecule in B8— selected not because it was among the brightest but because it was among the most novel—and feed it back into the AI, asking for ninety-six more variants of it. One of those, it turned out, was bright enough to be usable in research.

But imagine if EvolutionaryScale were screening new drugs. Every molecule the AI suggests must still be tested in cells, then in animals, and eventually in people, just like any other drug. Even the most sophisticated AI is only a partial simulator of the endlessly complicated world of molecular biology. It can make us faster, but it cannot replace the core functions of bench scientists.

The Twenty-Third Law of AI:
The most powerful AIs for advancing the frontiers of human knowledge can help us move faster, but they cannot replace experimentation in the real world.

AI for creating new organic molecules embodies the central paradox of all AI: It will be transformative, but in ways that are for the most part small. It's only in the steady accumulation of small transformations, the bootstrapping that takes place when technologies become infrastructure and pile one atop another, that AI can become something truly meaningful to the human race.

I've saved Rives for the last chapter because he's the best at describing, in a way both specific and gnomic, grounding and inspiring, the structures we are actually creating when we train a gigantic AI. Because what we are really making, in addition to a list of millions of rules for manipulating data, is a map of the relationships among all the bits of information an AI has learned.

As outlined in chapter 4, a large language model is a vector database containing all the words and most of the concepts in a particular language. It is an endless library with halls and stacks stretching to the horizon in every direction at once, in which the identities of all things exist entirely—and solely—in terms of their relationships to those of all other things. From this comes its power to operate on language in a way that resembles meaning. I say "resembles" because the things a large language model "knows" have no referents in the real world, the way you and I would think of them. No large language model is as yet attached to the kind of sensorimotor system required to connect these concepts to objects in the real world, nor the kind of three-dimensional world models in which we are able to interact with objects, both in real life and in our mind's eye.

"I think about language modeling as a form of self supervision," said Rives, who worked at Facebook AI for three years and completed a PhD at New York University, where Yann LeCun was one of his advisers. "So what that means is that we're predicting parts of the data from other parts of the data. And what this is really training the model to do is to learn to complete patterns in the data, given their context. There are different theories for why this may work, and it's not fully understood. But you know, what we see across artificial intelligence is that when you train a model to predict patterns at scale, information materializes within the parameters of the network that correlates with the underlying structure of the data."

However they're doing it, today's transformer-based AIs are uncovering hidden structures in data—what computer scientists call its latent structure. However imperfectly, they are discovering secret connections between one thing and another, yielding a sort of machine intuition. All models are wrong, including this one, but some are useful. And with time and patience and the march of algorithms, microchips, and techniques for gathering data, they can be refined.

"You can really think about these models, I think, in some sense, as inverting patterns in the data to discover the structure that gives rise to them," Rives continued. Proteins are written in an alphabet, like words, though nature has only twenty amino acids with which to "spell" them. The similarity to language is obvious but superficial. "The text of a protein sequence describes the chemical structure of a molecule, but at the very deepest level, there's a fundamental information relationship which links the biological properties of a protein to the patterns in its sequence, and this information relationship is the selection of protein sequences by evolution. And so for this reason, there's an image of biology that is encoded into the patterns and protein sequences."

Proteins can be enormous. The largest one ever characterized, PKZILLA-1, is an enzyme that makes poison for the algae *Prymnesium parvum*, which lives in brackish water and is a hazard to fish and other wildlife. PKZILLA-1, a name inspired by the movie monster Godzilla, is 34,000 amino acids long. And while the average protein is far smaller—less than 500—the possibility of nearly any of 20 amino acids appearing at any of those 500 to 34,000 positions means that there are more possible proteins than there are atoms in the universe, by many orders of magnitude.

Yet the order in which the amino acid building blocks of a protein can be arranged is, compared to that number, constrained by the necessities of life. "You can imagine that these models, in completing across patterns, across millions or billions of protein sequences, would discover that underlying structure which is determining which amino acids evolution can choose."

To imagine a library bigger than our universe—bigger than a

million universes—stuffed with tomes describing the structure of the most basic molecules that make up every organic thing from the tiniest virus to the mightiest whale, makes the mind fizz with excitement. It implies a volume of data so much larger than the largest repositories yet used to train today's AIs that it suggests that biology, unlike language, is an area in which what are known as scaling laws might still be at work.

Scaling laws are the idea, dominant for the first couple of years after the debut of ChatGPT, that simply cramming more data into AIs would make them ever more capable. Instead, model builders found that beyond a certain size, language models did not become more capable in ways that were meaningful for their end users. It's not clear why that happened; it might be that there simply wasn't enough high-quality data to be had, or it might be the result of limitations inherent in the underlying architecture of today's AIs. If it's the former, Rives may be right when he says that ever-bigger models for coming up with new proteins may prove to be more capable than today's. Even if that's not the case, the models his company—and researchers in many other companies—have already built are just beginning to be leveraged to accelerate the kind of science we'll need more of in the twenty-first century: research on new medicines, new treatments, and new enzymes that could lead to future breakthroughs for energy and materials science.

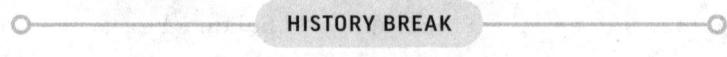

HISTORY BREAK

Huang's Law

There is a thing in technology known as Moore's Law, named for Intel cofounder Gordon Moore, which is often mischaracterized. First, like the many laws in this book, it's not a law; it's an observation about a set of conditions that were in existence for about fifty years, up until the late 2010s. Colloquially, it was known as the tendency for the power of the primary chips inside PCs—CPUs—to double in power every eighteen months or so. Economically, it was a description of the way that the number of transistors—the microscopic switches that do the processing on a microchip—that could be bought for a dollar doubled over the same period. And formally, in the chip-manufacturing industry, it was a description of the fact that every year or two, the number of transistors that could fit into a square millimeter doubled. All of those numbers are, or at least were, directly related, and the whole thing was driven by advances in the technology for projecting ever more finely detailed images of semiconductors onto silicon wafers and then forming transistors there through a process that was basically photographic.

Moore's Law ceased to apply, depending on whom you ask, sometime around 2016 or maybe as late as the early 2020s. The main reason was that shrinking the features on a microchip—the transistors, as well as the channels that ferry electrons among them—had bumped up against a fundamental limit, namely, the size of the atom. As of this writing, the most advanced microchips produced anywhere on planet Earth are made by TSMC Fabs in a factory, known as a fab, in Tainan Science Park on the southwest corner of Taiwan.

The smallest elements on these "3-nanometer" chips are 24 nanometers across, which in terms of crystalline silicon, is about 80 silicon atoms across. TSMC has plans for 2-nanometer chips and beyond, but there just aren't that many atoms left to shave off. Plus, below a certain size, electrons cease behaving in predictable ways, literally "tunneling" through barriers in a bit of quantum weirdness, leading to all kinds of potential errors. (From the perspective of our non-quantum senses, it's a form of teleportation.)

None of what I've just outlined is controversial. But what is controversial is whether or not Moore's Law is technically over, because computers keep getting faster. *Especially* the ones driving AI.

That's why in 2020, I coined the term Huang's Law, after NVIDIA CEO Jensen Huang, to describe the new scaling law driving what were already—and continue to be—very rapid increases in the power of the specialized chips behind today's AIs. Or at least, I thought I was coining the term. Later, I discovered that there was some prior art in the form of a prescient article by *IEEE Spectrum*'s Tekla Perry, the "Doyenne of the Valley" (Silicon Valley, that is). In any case, Huang's Law has had its own Wikipedia page since two days after I first wrote about it in 2020, which is now richly adorned with citations of subsequent discussions of this law, so I will take credit for being if not its originator, its hype man.

But what is Huang's Law? Put simply, it's the much-faster-than-every-eighteen-months doubling of the *performance* of the specialized chips for executing the calculations necessary for AI, which is due as much to optimizations in the ways chips are designed as to any upgrades in their physical—that is, Moore's Law–driven—substrate.

The reason any of this matters is that Huang's Law is a primary reason why AI keeps getting cheaper. NVIDIA's future "AI supercomputers," which the company has promised to build entirely in Texas, are assembled from chips that are not two times but *ten times* faster at running today's AIs than the last generation. NVIDIA is not alone. In early 2025, Google announced that its latest specialized chip for AI processing, what it calls a TPU, is 3,600 times faster than the chip it unveiled in 2017. What this means is that in the intervening eight years, the performance of Google's AI chips roughly *tripled every year.* That's Huang's Law at work.

One thing it's important to understand about Huang's Law is that it can't continue forever. I won't make a fool of myself by trying to predict when it will run out of steam, because I'm no expert in the innovations in integrating memory directly into these chips that are now the primary drivers of their increases in performance, when they're used to deliver to end users (as opposed to training) AIs. But just as surely as Moore's Law ran up against the hard limits of the physical world, Huang's Law will, too. Indeed, the massive power demands of today's data centers and the need for innovative ways to cool today's "AI supercomputers," forcing providers to switch from air-cooling to water-cooling and even immersion-cooling systems, illustrate that all this AI processing power is already coming at a price.

One thing a particular kind of AI booster has been fond of saying is that whatever AI model you're using on a given day, that's the worst version of it that will ever exist. Whether or not that's true—the plateauing performance of many models and the failure to get better results out of them by simply making them bigger makes it questionable—one thing that is absolutely the case is that AI will continue to become both faster and cheaper to deliver. Huang's Law virtually guarantees a future in which AI is a commodity, available on every device as well as in the cloud.

> After a year of philosophy, I switched again, my third year, I did psychology. I was extremely discontented with psychology. I guess what I was discontented about was they didn't seem to have any good models of anything. I expected them to have models of how the mind worked. And they didn't. Instead of thinking how the mind worked, it did things like rats in mazes. . . . I organized the other students to protest about the content of the course.
>
> —Geoffrey Hinton, *Talking Nets:*
> *An Oral History of Neural Network Research*

Rick Stevens is the AI guy at one of the most storied government laboratories on the planet: Argonne National Laboratory. The world has functioning nuclear power plants because of the work done at Argonne; it was born of the work of Enrico Fermi during World War II, when he worked on the Manhattan Project. Argonne also has what was briefly the world's fastest supercomputer, Aurora, built with taxpayer money for the fantastical price of $500 million.

Though it was completed in 2023, devices such as this one can seem like something out of a bygone age. In an era when Amazon, Microsoft, Google, and Meta collectively spent close to $300 billion in 2025 on data centers and their support infrastructure, publicly funded supercomputers usable for scientific research can seem quaint. But as the nature of AI research changes— breakthroughs that were once shared widely are now kept behind closed doors, and universities where researchers once did pioneering work are now hemorrhaging PhDs, thanks to companies offering salaries in the millions of dollars—this kind of public AI infrastructure has become all the more important. All the evidence, from companies such as EvolutionaryScale and the public science still being done by Google DeepMind to the sharp increase in research done at public universities aided by AI, suggests that many of the biggest impacts of this technology over the course of the twenty-first century will be in science, especially basic scientific research.

Some of this will happen on account of science being the kind of knowledge work for which AI is a perfect fit. For example, numerous scientific search engines that leverage LLMs and semantic search have popped up in the past few years, including Scite and Consensus. Deep-research tools are particularly well suited to digging up and summarizing papers and data that would otherwise take hours of work with conventional search engines and reading papers on one's own. And the ability to ask questions of scientific papers, which are notoriously impenetrable, after uploading them to AI tools, is the kind of game changer that has to be experienced to be fully appreciated. In all of these roles, AI as it's being used in businesses the world over is now table stakes for scientific research. In a field that makes such extraordinary demands on its practitioners—to know as much as possible, to make connections across that knowledge, and to keep up with others who are racing ahead with their own work— using AI as a bicycle for the mind is already, and nearly universally, standard practice.

At Argonne, there are already hundreds of scientists using commercial AI reasoning models to assist their work, said Stevens. But what he's really excited about are the laboratory's efforts to use AI in science that are far more ambitious.

Some of those efforts consist of taking conventional models

based on traditional physics and fluid dynamics—think of a weather model—and training gigantic deep learning systems on their outputs. This is no mere parlor trick; such systems can actually outperform the conventional models they're trained on. What in any other age would have made headlines as a big advance on account of AI—the debut of Google DeepMind's GenCast model in late 2024—debuted with hardly any notice on account of the concurrent hype for AI chatbots and the impending inauguration of a certain president.

What GenCast accomplished was a substantial improvement on fifteen-day weather forecasts generated by the best weather forecasters using conventional models. These kinds of forecasts, of not just conventional weather but also deadly storms, are essential for preparing people for deadly weather. GenCast's advances on the state of the art were so notable that the European Centre for Medium-Range Weather Forecasts, regarded as the world's most accurate long-range weather forecasting organization, has incorporated some of its techniques into its modeling.

This process of replacing conventional models with simplified emulators of them, built by training AI on the outputs of those models or, as in the case of weather models, on decades of historical data, is called "surrogate modeling." "In high-performance computing over the past five to six years, there has been an enormous amount of progress with surrogate models," said Stevens. "In many cases this works quite well, and you can produce an output—a weather forecast, the electronic structure estimate of a band gap in a material—with similar or better accuracy than the original model." Even better, these systems are vastly less costly to run, in terms of computer cycles and therefore time and electricity, than conventional ones. "You get enormous acceleration, because the machine-learned kernels are orders of magnitude more computationally efficient than solving the original partial differential equations," he added. Groups at Argonne are using such models for material science, chemistry, quantum materials design, weather and climate forecasting, imaging, and even neuroscience.

The other big area in which AI is accelerating scientific discovery is in code generation, said Stevens. "Everything we do in science these days involves writing code, right? Writing your code for simulations or code for data analysis or code for manipulating data or code for controlling instruments or whatever. You're just always writing code. You can't really be a modern scientist without being able to write code; even if you're an experimentalist or a theorist, you're going to be writing code all the time."

I've mostly avoided talking about perhaps the single best use of generative AI for the entirety of this book—writing code—for one simple reason: People who are savvy enough to use AI to write code probably don't need to read a book on how to use AI to make themselves more productive. Anything I say on the subject will be hopelessly out of date by the time anyone reads this, and the internet, being the natural home of the technologically astute, is a far better teacher on this matter than I could ever hope to be. But it's worth acknowledging that AI-powered code-writing tools are the area developing fastest in all of AI, for two reasons: First, writing code is an amazing fit for a system that is best at providing examples of what everyone else has written before. Good programming is, after all, often about writing as little code as possible and focusing on the architecture of systems using the best code already written by others.

Then there's the way that code, like mathematics, is uniquely suited to the abilities of the latest and most powerful AI reasoning models. These models are trained through reinforcement learning to provide correct responses to queries. In both code and math, there is often one correct or at least consensus answer, something that is hardly true in any other endeavor. This means that reasoning models keep getting better at doing coding and math in a way that they aren't getting better—and in some ways lately have gotten worse—at performing other tasks.

"We're starting to see a shift towards almost everybody who's seriously doing code development using models in some augmented way, including, I mean, myself," said Stevens. "I write code every day, and my productivity has gone up by a factor of ten at least, maybe, maybe even more. I can routinely generate two or three hundred lines of code in ten or fifteen minutes using a model, and before it would take me, you know, a day or two doing it without a model." These same models speed up the development process in other ways, by helping to debug code, optimize code, or translate it so that it can operate in a different computing environment.

The Twenty-Fourth Law of AI: The field of human endeavor most transformed by generative AI is coding.

So then we got very excited, because now there was this very simple local learning rule. On paper it looked just great. I mean, you could take this great big network, and you could train up all the weights to do just the right thing, just with a simple local learning rule. It felt like we'd solved the problem. That must be how the brain works. I guess if it hadn't been for computer simulations, I'd still believe that.

—Geoffrey Hinton, *Talking Nets: An Oral History of Neural Network Research*

In early 2025, a report from inside OpenAI leaked the news that the company had contemplated charging $20,000 a month for an AI agent capable of supporting "PhD-level research." While such an agent might be good for the company's bottom line, all evidence suggests that the biggest competition for such an agent will be a human, augmented by the reasoning models provided by OpenAI itself.

Scientists are beginning to use AI models as part of their ideation and innovation process in a kind of God-tier version of the same process that a company such as Clorox uses them to help come up with new consumer goods. Say, for example, you're a scientist interested in a new kind of metallo-organic framework for catalysis. Translation: You want to use a material so novel and advanced that it's never escaped the lab and been commercialized to facilitate chemical reactions that could be critical for, say, next-generation batteries for faster-charging and more affordable electric vehicles.

"You might start by saying, well, okay, there's a literature on this," said Stevens. "There's dozens of papers, and there's experimental techniques, analytical techniques, and so on for understanding these things. As a working scientist, you might say, 'Well, okay, how do I explore some new possible approach to doing this?' And it turns out that you can start chatting with models about this deep area and ask them to consider alternative approaches and have them derive, say, the physical statement that describes that problem."

While today's reasoning models aren't nearly as creative as people, they've read and memorized literally *all* the literature, which means that scientists can talk through a problem and use them to explore alternative ideas. "If they're paired up with a clever scientist who's willing to explore with them, you can get much further as a partnership with the AI than you can just working on your own," said Stevens. "We're starting to see that pan out, whether it's in cosmology, biochemistry, molecular biology, or other areas."

As with EvolutionaryScale's AI, which contains a library of all known molecules, modern reasoning models that contain a library of all available scientific papers differ from the kinds of AIs we encounter on a daily basis—chatbots, copilots, and the like—in that they can do something that no human could aspire to do. No scientist, no matter how learned, can do an approximate semantic search across all available literature on a subject. And while the rules of thumb these reasoning models have accumulated about the relationships among all of those scientific concepts might be primitive or in some cases less than completely accurate, the fact that they exist at all is a world-historic first.

This is just a guess, but I'd venture to say that there is already more latent knowledge inside the world's reasoning models trained on scientific papers than exists in the heads of all scientists alive today. This does not mean in any way that these models are smarter or more capable than all of those human scientists—just that they have, awaiting discovery in their vast cybernetic brains, more hidden connections among scientific concepts than any one scientist could ever hope to accrue, and a significant portion of the AI-assisted future of coming up with new scientific hypotheses will be about mining those ideas.

This leads me to the most important conclusion in this book and the most important law of AI. It's one you've heard before, but it bears repeating.

The First Law of AI:
AI is an assistant, not a replacement.

The investments that the tech giants and some of the best-funded startups in history have made into physical infrastructure to train and deliver the most cutting-edge AIs, plus the unbelievable salaries and stock grants they have thrown at AI engineers in the most frenetic war for talent in the history of technology, mean that all of these companies are going to continue to push—hard—the idea that agentic AIs are replacements for human employees.

There simply isn't enough money in the world's corporate, small-business, and individual IT budgets to justify all of those customers spending at the level they would have to in order to provide the AI builders with the revenue required to justify their investments in data centers and talent.

And so the world's builders of AI are now looking at a different market. One well-known AI researcher just came out and said the quiet part out loud when, in the spring of 2025, he announced a new startup, Mechanize, the goal of which was "the full automation of all work" and "the full automation of the economy." In other words, these companies' total addressable market has long since ceased to be the nearly $6 trillion everyone on Earth collectively spends on IT. Instead, it is becoming the approximately $100 trillion a year the world pays itself in wages and salaries.

Coupled with this economic driver of tech companies' estimates of the value of their AI agents is the ongoing overconfidence in the rate of advance in their abilities. Every year, some combination of Sam Altman of OpenAI, Dario Amodei of Anthropic, Demis Hassabis of Google DeepMind, and Elon Musk promise that artificial general intelligence—human-level abilities in an AI—will arrive somewhere between one and ten years from now. Combine this with a steady flow of ever-more-convincing depictions of AGI in the movies and television shows we're all being fed, and it's no wonder that 68 percent of American adults told the Pew Research Center in 2025 that they believed AI would have a negative or at best neutral effect on the world over the next twenty years.

I believe that much of this anxiety boils down to the effects of AI on employment and wages and that it is a consequence of pronouncements that are, in a word, bunk. If you take one thing away from this book, let it be this: Like all previous forms of automation, AI is a tool. It can ease our burdens and increase our productivity, and it may help us achieve new breakthroughs in the areas where we'll need them most in the twenty-first century, from energy and medicine to robotics and national security—but it's a tool nonetheless.

TERMS

Evolutionary scale model (ESM): A transformer-based model in which all relevant data about a protein—its sequence, structure, and function—has been turned into tokens so that the AI can learn from it. For amino acids, which are already a kind of alphabet, this is trivial. But for the three-dimensional structure of the proteins they make up, researchers had to figure out a way to translate them into a kind of alphabet.

Latent structure: The hidden structure of a pool of data, which today's AI models have some ability to divine and store in the latent—or hidden—parameters in the many in-between layers of their deep learning networks.

Scaling laws: The idea that as a model grows bigger, it becomes more capable. Much of the boom in AI investment of the early to mid-2020s was predicated on the idea that these laws would hold for far longer than they did.

Moore's Law: The idea that every eighteen months or so, the number of transistors on a microchip would double and its performance would increase proportionally but the cost of the microchip would stay the same. Named for Gordon Moore, the founder of Intel, it lasted for about fifty years and ended in about 2016.

Huang's Law: Named after NVIDIA founder Jensen Huang, Huang's Law is much more about optimizations in the design of microchips. It's lasted nearly six years and shows no signs of becoming obsolete, although inevitably it will be someday.

Surrogate models: The replacement of conventional mathematical models of physical and other processes with AI-based ones trained on the outputs of those models or on historical data. Surrogate models can be both more accurate and far less expensive to run. A primary example is new AI-powered weather models.

SUMMARY

What to Know

Many of the biggest changes in our lives brought about by AI will be on account of the way it is already accelerating scientific research.

How to Think About It

As with all AI hype, you should be skeptical of anyone insisting that AI will radically transform something as complicated and multicausal as the pace of scientific research. But science, engineering, and coding are the three fields that stand to benefit most from AI. This means that the most significant impact of AI on all our lives is almost certainly going to be indirect and invisible.

What Questions to Ask

When AI promises to accelerate some phases of the process of research and development, what proportion of the total time required do those phases actually represent? What pools of unstructured or semistructured data are yet untapped for training new AIs, and are there companies already attempting to use them? In a contest between an AI agent and a human augmented by AI, which is more productive, accurate, and useful?

Acknowledgments

For a book like this to exist, dozens, possibly hundreds, of people have been generous with their knowledge, patiently tutoring me in what they do and how they think about it. Whenever I reflect on what goes into a reporting project like this, I'm astonished that so many of the smartest and most capable people on Earth are so generous with the most precious resource they have: time. Every named source in this book has my eternal gratitude for sharing their wisdom with me. I'm no less grateful to the many others who have educated me about AI over the years and whose know-how is in this book, even if they aren't.

I'm also extremely grateful to my editors at *The Wall Street Journal,* who have been my intellectual companions on this journey, working through countless drafts of stories on AI and asking the probing questions that have forced me to go deeper. Jason Dean, Tom Gryta, Emily Nelson, Erik Holm, Ethan Smith, Liz Rappaport, Wilson Rothman, and Jamie Heller all deserve my thanks, as do close to a dozen other editors who have commissioned or weighed in on a piece on AI at one time or another.

Here's where I get to credit my otherwise uncredited coauthors. First there's agent extraordinaire Rafe Sagalyn, who is the only one who knows how many other books had to be pitched and then cast aside in order to finally arrive at the right one for this moment. And then there's Paul Whitlatch, my editor at Crown, who had more good ideas than I could count, knows how to work magic on a deadline, and somehow made this process much more fun than writing this many words has a right to be.

Then there's my extended-family support network, all the members of whom have helped me by taking on burdens of one kind or another so that I could carve out the time to write this book. The village with whom I raise our kids—the family and friends of greater Dickeyville (and its suburbs, known to most people as Baltimore)—is incredible, and I love you all. I know that most of them would prefer to remain anonymous, but special thanks goes to my sisters. This book—and all of my books— would not exist without Amanda Shepherd, the uncredited coauthor of every aspect of our shared life.

Finally, I don't know how I could have done this without the two smartest, most empathetic, and most patient sounding boards for ideas I've ever met, Leo Mirani and John Pavlus.

Notes

INTRODUCTION: THE ORIGINAL SINS OF ARTIFICIAL INTELLIGENCE

xiii   **In November 2022:** Jem Bartholomew and Dhrumil Mehta, "How the Media Is Covering ChatGPT," *Columbia Journalism Review*, May 26, 2023. https://www.cjr.org/tow_center/media-coverage-chatgpt.php.

xiii   **At a series of meetings:** Stephanie Dick, "Of Models and Machines: Implementing Bounded Rationality," *Isis* 106, no. 3 (September 2015): 623–34, https://doi.org/10.1086/683527.

xiii   **"complex information processing":** Herbert A. Simon and Allen Newell, "Information Processing in Computer and Man," *American Scientist* 52, no. 3 (September 1964): 281–300.

xiv   **On that day in late November 2022:** Bartholomew and Mehta, "How the Media Is Covering ChatGPT."

xiv   **"Fourth Industrial Revolution":** Klaus Schwab, "The Fourth Industrial Revolution: What It Means, How to Respond," World Economic Forum, January 14, 2016, https://www.weforum.org/stories/2016/01/the-fourth-industrial-revolution-what-it-means-and-how-to-respond.

xvi   **It's what historians call:** Beth Stackpole, "The Impact of Generative AI as a General-Purpose Technology," MIT Sloan School of Management, August 6, 2024, https://mitsloan.mit.edu/ideas-made-to-matter/impact-generative-ai-a-general-purpose-technology.

1. DON'T PANIC

4   **a New York judge fined:** Sara Merken, "New York lawyers sanctioned for using fake ChatGPT cases in legal brief," Reuters, June 26, 2023, https://www.reuters.com/legal/new-york-lawyers-sanctioned-using-fake-chatgpt-cases-legal-brief-2023-06-22/.

7   **jobs that companies outsourced:** James Manyika et al., "Jobs Lost, Jobs Gained: What the Future of Work Will Mean for Jobs, Skills, and Wages," McKinsey & Company, November 28, 2017, https://www.mckinsey.com/featured-insights/future-of-work/jobs-lost-jobs-gained-what-the-future-of-work-will-mean-for-jobs-skills-and-wages#.

8   **the more you can get out:** Ethan Mollick, "15 Times to Use AI, and 5 Not To," One Useful Thing, December 9, 2024, https://www.oneusefulthing .org/p/15-times-to-use-ai-and-5-not-to.

10   **Sam Altman memorably put it:** Scott Rosenberg, "Altman's Hazy AI Utopia," Axios, September 25, 2024, https://www.axios.com/2024/09/25/ openai-sam-altman-ai-intelligence-age.

2. KEEP CALM AND EMBRACE AI

14   **plummeted by nearly 20 percent:** "Freelance Forward 2023," Upwork, December 12, 2023, https://www.upwork.com/research/freelance -forward-2023-research-report; Ozge Demirci, Jonas Hannane, and Xinrong Zhu, "Who Is AI Replacing? The Impact of Generative AI on Online Freelancing Platforms," SSRN, February 21, 2024, https:// papers.ssrn.com/sol3/Delivery.cfm/4602944.pdf?abstractid=4602944 &mirid=1.

15   **a drop in demand:** Jin Liu et al., "'Generate' the Future of Work Through AI: Empirical Evidence from Online Labor Markets," arXiv, June 18, 2025, https://arxiv.org/abs/2308.05201.

27   **"living algorithms":** Alan Burdick, "How Fungi Move Among Us," *The New York Times,* March 1, 2025, https://www.nytimes.com/2025/03/01/ science/climate-mycorrhizal-fungus-networks.html.

32   **Machine psychology:** Thilo Hagendorff et al., "Machine Psychology," arXiv, August 8, 2024, https://arxiv.org/abs/2303.13988.

3. AI IS JUST SOFTWARE

35   **never touched an AI chatbot:** Lee Rainie, "Close Encounters of the AI Kind," Elon University, March 12, 2025, https://imaginingthedigitalfuture .org/reports-and-publications/close-encounters-of-the-ai-kind.

35   **By the end of 2024:** Matt G. Southern, "Study: Google AI Overviews Appear in 47% of Search Results," Search Engine Journal, December 11, 2024, https://www.searchenginejournal.com/study-google-ai-overviews -appear-in-47-of-search-results/535096.

38   **"Big company–itis":** Jordan Novet, "Google A.I. Researcher Says He Left to Build a Startup After Encountering 'Big Company–itis,'" CNBC, August 17, 2023, https://www.cnbc.com/2023/08/17/transformer-co -author-llion-jones-leaves-google-for-startup-sakana-ai.html.

38   **a 2017 article:** Ashish Vaswani et al., "Attention Is All You Need," arXiv, August 2, 2023, https://arxiv.org/abs/1706.03762.

38   **All but one of them:** "6 Authors of a Seminal Research Paper by Google

That Helped Enable OpenAI Have Raised $1.3B in Startup Funding and Already Created 2 Unicorns," CB Insights, April 7, 2023, https://www .cbinsights.com/research/google-transformer-startups-openai.

38   **forked over $2.7 billion:** Miles Kruppa and Lauren Thomas, "Google Paid $2.7 Billion to Bring Back an AI Genius Who Quit in Frustration," *The Wall Street Journal,* September 25, 2024, https://www.wsj.com/tech/ ai/noam-shazeer-google-ai-deal-d3605697.

39   **the company incorporated BERT:** Steven Levy, "8 Google Employees Invented Modern AI. Here's the Inside Story," Wired, March 20, 2024, https://www.wired.com/story/eight-google-employees-invented-modern -ai-transformers-paper.

4. AI AS PERSONAL RESEARCH ASSISTANT AND LIBRARIAN

51   **those in the latter group:** Travis Dixon, "Key Study: Gandhi and the Anchoring Effect," IB Psychology, March 30, 2020, https://www .themantic-education.com/ibpsych/2020/03/10/key-study-ghandi-and -the-anchoring-effect.

51   **if you try to debunk:** Briony Swire-Thompson, Joseph DeGutis, and David Lazer, "Searching for the Backfire Effect: Measurement and Design Considerations," *Journal of Applied Research in Memory and Cognition* 9, no. 3 (September 2020): 286–99, https://doi.org/10.1016/j .jarmac.2020.06.006.

53   **all used algorithms:** Mark Gales and Steve Young, "The Application of Hidden Markov Models in Speech Recognition," *Foundations and Trends in Signal Processing* 1, no. 3 (2007): 195–304, https://doi.org/ 10.1561/9781601981219.

53   **transformers performed much better:** Ashish Vaswani et al., "Attention Is All You Need," arXiv, August 2, 2023, https://arxiv.org/abs/1706 .03762.

54   **Both comprehension and production:** Pranav Dixit, "OpenAI Claims That Its Free GPT-4o Model Can Talk, Laugh, Sing and See Like a Human," Engadget, May 13, 2024, https://www.engadget.com/openai -claims-that-its-free-gpt-4o-model-can-talk-laugh-sing-and-see-like-a -human-184249780.html.

54   **It helped that the voice:** Dan Milmo, "Scarlett Johansson's OpenAI Clash Is Just the Start of Legal Wrangles over Artificial Intelligence," *The Guardian,* May 27, 2024, https://www.theguardian.com/technology/ article/2024/may/27/scarlett-johansson-openai-legal-artificial -intelligence-chatgpt.

54   **"trained on 680,000 hours":** "Whisper: A multilingual and multitask robust ASR model," Shaped.ai, https://www.shaped.ai/blog/whisper-a -multilingual-and-multitask-robust-asr-model.

54   **much of the meeting transcription:** Otter.ai, "Otter.ai Brings New AI Capabilities to Zoom Customers at Zoomtopia," October 11, 2018, https://www.prweb.com/releases/otter-ai-brings-new-ai-capabilities-to -zoom-customers-at-zoomtopia-857430109.html.

57   **In mid-2023, Otter's capabilities:** "Otter AI Chat: More Intelligent and Collaborative than ChatGPT for Your Everyday Team Meetings," Otter, June 21, 2023, https://otter.ai/blog/otter-ai-chat-more-intelligent-and -collaborative-than-chatgpt-for-your-everyday-team-meetings.

58   **"semantic search":** Tiannuo Yang et al., "Demystifying and Enhancing the Efficiency of Large Language Model Based Search Agents," arXiv, May 17, 2025, https://arxiv.org/abs/2505.12065.

60   **Researchers have been doing:** "A Guide on Word Embeddings in NLP," Turing, February 10, 2022, https://www.turing.com/kb/guide-on-word -embeddings-in-nlp.

5. THE FIRST EMBERS OF AGENTIC AI

78   **"garbage in, garbage out":** Richard Sheposh, "Garbage In, Garbage Out (GIGO)," EBSCO Information Services, 2024, https://www.ebsco.com/ research-starters/computer-science/garbage-garbage-out-gigo.

78   **it will decline to answer them:** Brett Ashley Crawford, "NotebookLM: A Reliable Knowledge Partner," Arts Management & Technology Laboratory, Carnegie Mellon University, February 20, 2025, https://amt -lab.org/reviews/2025/2/notebooklm-a-reliable-knowledge-partner.

79   **Alan Turing publishes:** "Lovelace, Turing and the Invention of Computers," Science Museum, December 14, 2018, https://www .sciencemuseum.org.uk/objects-and-stories/lovelace-turing-and -invention-computers.

79   **world's first neural network–based device:** "Rosenblatt's Perceptron Uses a Type of Neural Network," Jeremy Norman's HistoryofInformation .com, https://www.historyofinformation.com/detail.php?id=770.

80   **Marvin Minsky and Seymour Papert publish:** Marvin L. Minsky and Seymour A. Papert, *Perceptrons: An Introduction to Computational Geometry* (Cambridge, Mass.: MIT Press, 1969).

80   **Kunihiko Fukushima, a researcher:** "Kunihiko Fukushima," The Franklin Institute, March 2020, https://fi.edu/en/awards/laureates/kunihiko -fukushima.

80   **Yann LeCun, one of the "godfathers":** Yann LeCun et al., "Gradient-Based Learning Applied to Document Recognition," *Proceedings of the*

IEEE 86, no. 11 (November 1998): 2278–324, https://doi.org/10.1109/
5.726791.

80   **associates and students of Geoffrey Hinton:** "7.1. Deep Convolutional
Neural Networks (AlexNet)," Dive into Deep Learning, https://classic
.d2l.ai/chapter_convolutional-modern/alexnet.html.

80   **Google's AlphaGo beats the world's best player:** "AlphaGo," Google
DeepMind, https://deepmind.google/research/projects/alphago.

80   **Researchers at Google publish:** Ashish Vaswani et al., "Attention Is
All You Need," arXiv, August 2, 2023, https://arxiv.org/abs/1706
.03762.

80   **Google starts using:** Bill Ross, "Google's BERT Update Explained and
Recovery Strategies," Emulent, December 21, 2024, https://emulent.com/
blog/googles-bert-update-explained-and-recovery-strategies.

80   **GitHub's Copilot becomes:** Karl Montevirgen, "OpenAI," Britannica
Money, June 19, 2025, https://www.britannica.com/money/OpenAI.

81   **Devin AI debuts:** Sramana Mitra, "Agentic AI: Cognition AI Soars on
Devin's Success," One Million by One Million Blog, March 14, 2025,
https://www.sramanamitra.com/2025/03/14/agentic-ai-cognition-ai
-soars-on-devins-success.

81   **The first deep-research tool:** Atikah Amalia, "Google Rolls Out Free
Features in Gemini, Including Deep Research Tool," ContentGrip,
March 18, 2025, https://www.contentgrip.com/google-gemini-ai-free
-deep-research-tool.

83   **Almost all data needed:** Mario Dudjak, "Data Preprocessing: The
Backbone of AI and ML," FERIT.ai, April 9, 2025, https://ferit.ai/data
-preprocessing-the-backbone-of-ai-and-ml.

83   **something like 90 percent:** Ravi Malick, "90% of Your Data Is
Unstructured—and It's Full of Untapped Value," Box Blogs, August 24,
2023, https://blog.box.com/90-your-data-unstructured-and-its-full
-untapped-value.

87   **economists were baffled:** Stuart MacDonald, Pat Anderson, and Dieter
Kimbel, "Measurement or Management?: Revisiting the Productivity
Paradox of Information Technology," *Vierteljahrshefte zur
Wirtschaftsforschung* 69, no. 4 (2000): 601–17, https://www.econstor.eu/
bitstream/10419/99168/1/vjh.69.4.601.pdf.

6. AI FOR CREATIVITY

94   **"multimodal image generation":** Jing Yu Koh, Daniel Fried, and Ruslan
Salakhutdinov, "Generating Images with Multimodal Language
Models," arXiv, October 13, 2023, https://arxiv.org/abs/2305.17216.

95   **is on a par with putting a question:** Will Grannis, "2025 and the Next

Chapter(s) of AI," Google, January 16, 2025, https://cloud.google.com/transform/2025-and-the-next-chapters-of-ai.

97   the simultaneous arrival: Annabelle Nyst, "History of ChatGPT: A Timeline of the Meteoric Rise of Generative AI Chatbots," Search Engine Journal, October 9, 2024, https://www.searchenginejournal.com/history-of-chatgpt-timeline/488370.

98   Periods of relative stasis are followed: Keith D. Foote, "A Brief History of Generative AI," Dataversity, March 5, 2024, https://www.dataversity.net/a-brief-history-of-generative-ai.

99   Founded in 1913: "Timeline," The Clorox Company, https://www.thecloroxcompany.com/company/our-story/timeline.

102 many photographers and videographers are turning: "Benefits of Using Virtual Production for Photography," Ramaz Studios, https://ramazstudios.com/benefits-of-virtual-production-for-photography.

103 the *Mandalorian* series: Industrial Light & Magic. "The Virtual Production of The Mandalorian Season One," YouTube, February 20, 2020, https://www.youtube.com/watch?v=gUnxzVOs3rk.

7. "CLASSIC" AI

110 One of the jokes about AI: Benjamin Bratton, "The Five Stages of AI Grief," Noema, June 20, 2024, https://www.noemamag.com/the-five-stages-of-ai-grief.

110 Above a certain temperature: Hayon Michelle Choi et al., "Temperature, Crime, and Violence: A Systematic Review and Meta-Analysis," *Environmental Health Perspectives* 132, no. 10 (October 15, 2024), https://doi.org/10.1289/ehp14300.

111 A later version, the Mark I: Frank Rosenblatt, *Principles of Neurodynamics: Perceptrons and the Theory of Brain Mechanisms* (Cornell Aeronautical Laboratory, 1961), https://archive.org/details/DTIC_AD0256582/mode/2up.

112 wasn't fast enough: Vivek Singh, "Game-Changer: How the World's First GPU Leveled Up Gaming and Ignited the AI Era," NVIDIA, October 11, 2024, https://blogs.nvidia.com/blog/first-gpu-gaming-ai.

113 coauthored a book: Marvin L. Minsky and Seymour A. Papert, *Perceptrons: An Introduction to Computational Geometry* (Cambridge, Mass.: MIT Press, 1969).

117 came up with the idea: Anna Davour, "They Used Physics to Find Patterns in Information," The Royal Swedish Academy of Sciences, 2024, https://www.nobelprize.org/uploads/2024/11/popular-physicsprize2024-3.pdf.

118 Hinton didn't join Google: Robert McMillan, "Google Hires Brains That

Helped Supercharge Machine Learning," Wired, March 13, 2013, https://www.wired.com/2013/03/google-hinton.

118   **overreliance on it was one reason:** Vern L. Glaser, Omid Omidvar, and Mehdi Safavi, "Predictive Models Can Lose the Plot. Here's How to Keep Them on Track," *MIT Sloan Management Review,* June 13, 2023, https://sloanreview.mit.edu/article/predictive-models-can-lose-the-plot -heres-how-to-keep-them-on-track.

8. AI FOR INNOVATION

129   **they actually seemed to be better ideas:** Ethan Mollick, "How to . . . Use AI to Generate Ideas," One Useful Thing, December 3, 2022, https://www.oneusefulthing.org/p/how-to-use-ai-to-generate-ideas.

130   **idea generation benefits:** Paul Paulus and Huei-Chuan Yang, "Idea Generation in Groups: A Basis for Creativity in Organizations," *Organizational Behavior and Human Decision Processes* 82, no. 1 (May 2000): 76–87, https://doi.org/10.1006/obhd.2000.2888.

130   **Their experiment included:** Ethan Mollick, "The Cybernetic Teammate," One Useful Thing, March 22, 2025, https://www.oneusefulthing.org/p/the-cybernetic-teammate.

130   **AI came up with better ideas:** Christian Terwiesch and Karl Ulrich, "M.B.A. Students vs. AI: Who Comes Up with More Innovative Ideas?," *The Wall Street Journal,* September 9, 2023, https://www.wsj.com/tech/ai/mba-students-vs-chatgpt-innovation-679edf3b.

134   **they frequently make up:** "UTSA Researchers Investigate AI Threats in Software Development," UTSA Today, April 7, 2025, https://www.utsa .edu/today/2025/04/story/utsa-researchers-investigate-AI-threats.html.

134   **fill them with malicious code:** Solomon Klappholz, "Hackers Take Advantage of AI Hallucinations to Sneak Malicious Software Packages onto Enterprise Repositories," IT Pro, April 2, 2024, https://www.itpro .com/security/hackers-are-taking-advantage-of-ai-hallucinations-to -sneak-malicious-software-packages-onto-enterprise-repositories.

9. TAKE YOUR AI AGENT TO WORK DAY

137   **has actually *declined*:** Gina Potthoff Kacik, "US Construction Has a Productivity Problem," Chicago Booth Review, July 25, 2023, https://www.chicagobooth.edu/review/us-construction-has-productivity -problem.

138   **productivity grew by 2.1 percent:** Shawn Sprague, "The U.S. Productivity Slowdown: An Economy-Wide and Industry-Level Analysis," Monthly Labor Review, U.S. Bureau of Labor Statistics, April 2021, https://www

.bls.gov/opub/mlr/2021/article/the-us-productivity-slowdown-the
-economy-wide-and-industry-level-analysis.htm.

138   **is a major reason why:** Leonardo D'Amico et al., "Why Has
Construction Productivity Stagnated? The Role of Land-Use
Regulation," Cato Institute, March 12, 2025, https://www.cato.org/
research-briefs-economic-policy/why-has-construction-productivity
-stagnated#.

140   **Since about 2020:** "Introducing Root Cause Analysis and Additional A.I.
Capabilities," Procore, July 1, 2020, https://blog.procore.com/
introducing-root-cause-analysis-and-additional-ai-capabilities.

140   **In 2023, the company announced:** "Procore Revolutionizes Construction
Workflows with Innovative AI-Powered Copilot," Procore, September 19,
2023, https://www.procore.com/press/procore-revolutionizes
-construction-workflows-with-innovative-ai-powered-copilot.

144   **5 percent of the direct costs:** Duane Craig, "Most Common Rework
Causes and How to Prevent Them," Jobsite by Procore, June 4, 2018,
https://www.procore.com/jobsite/construction-rework-causes-costs.

146   **posted on Bluesky:** Dustin Moskovitz, "There are two clear power laws
already visible," Bluesky, March 31, 2025, https://bsky.app/profile/
moskov.goodventures.org/post/3llpngraais23.

147   **$20 for every million tokens:** Yolanda Gil and Raymond Perrault,
Artificial Intelligence Index Report 2025, Stanford University Human-
Centered Artificial Intelligence, 2025, https://hai.stanford.edu/assets/
files/hai_ai_index_report_2025.pdf.

147   **"What Lean did for manufacturing":** Christopher Mims, "The Secret
Weapon Helping Businesses Get Results from AI: Humans," *The Wall
Street Journal,* December 6, 2024, https://www.wsj.com/tech/ai/the
-secret-weapon-helping-businesses-get-results-from-ai-humans
-f99a0907.

148   **who represented Florida's 18th District:** "MURPHY, Patrick,"
Biographical Directory of the United States Congress, accessed June 05,
2025, https://bioguide.congress.gov/search/bio/M001191.

10. AI FOR DESKLESS WORKERS

153   **the other 37 percent:** MSL Staff, "One-Third of U.S. Workforce Missed
by Traditional Company Communications," MSL, March 15, 2022,
https://mslgroup.com/whats-new-at-msl/one-third-us-workforce-missed
-traditional-company-communications.

156   **"technology adoption life cycle":** Thierry Rayna, Ludmila Striukova, and
Samuel Landau, "Crossing the Chasm or Being Crossed Out: The Case
of Digital Audio Players," *International Journal of Actor-Network*

Theory and Technological Innovation 1, no. 3 (July–September 2009): 36–54, https://papers.ssrn.com/sol3/papers.cfm?abstract_id=1392691.

156   **obscure paper about farmers:** George M. Beal and Joe M. Bohlen, "The Diffusion Process," Agricultural Extension Service, Iowa State College, Ames, IA, March 1957, http://www.colligo.com/media/document/soc .iastate.edu_.SP18.pdf.

161   **In one of our conversations:** Christopher Mims and Tim Higgins, "Bold Names: The CEO Who Says Cheaper AI Could Actually Mean More Jobs," *The Wall Street Journal,* December 7, 2024.

161   **Here's what he wrote:** Aaron Levie, "The biggest opportunities in AI," X, December 5, 2024, https://x.com/levie/status/1864893134435684582.

163   **they cannot be the engines:** Belle Lin, "Why Amazon Is Betting on 'Automated Reasoning' to Reduce AI's Hallucinations," *The Wall Street Journal,* February 5, 2025, https://www.wsj.com/articles/why-amazon-is -betting-on-automated-reasoning-to-reduce-ais-hallucinations-b838849e.

164   **one of my colleagues polled:** Belle Lin, "AI Agents Are Everywhere . . . and Nowhere," *The Wall Street Journal,* February 12, 2025, https://www .wsj.com/articles/ai-agents-are-everywhereand-nowhere-87e38703.

11. WE, ROBOT

171   **On January 7, 2025:** Wency Chen, "CES 2025: Nvidia CEO Takes Centre Stage at CES with New Consumer GPU Card for Gaming, AI," *South China Morning Post,* January 7, 2025, https://www.scmp.com/tech/big -tech/article/3293740/ces-2025-nvidia-ceo-takes-centre-stage-new -consumer-graphics-card-gaming-ai.

172   **"The ChatGPT moment":** Christopher Mims, "Humanoid Robots Finally Get Real Jobs," *The Wall Street Journal,* February 26, 2025, https://www.wsj.com/tech/ai/humanoid-robot-workers-ai-brain -08027439.

175   **announced that it had raised $400 million:** "Robot AI Startup Physical Intelligence Raises $400 Mln from Bezos, OpenAI," Reuters, November 4, 2024, https://www.reuters.com/technology/artificial -intelligence/robot-ai-startup-physical-intelligence-raises-400-mln-bezos -openai-2024-11-04.

175   **Elon Musk said that Tesla:** Fred Lambert, "Elon Musk Says Tesla Aims to Build 10,000 Optimus Robots This Year," Electrek, January 31, 2025, https://electrek.co/2025/01/31/elon-musk-says-tesla-aims-to-build-10000 -optimus-robots-this-year.

175   **Figure was reportedly in talks:** Emily Glazer, Berber Jin, and Alexander Saeedy, "The $40 Billion Startup Mystery Shaking Up Silicon Valley," *The Wall Street Journal,* April 9, 2025, https://www.wsj.com/tech/the

-hottest-pre-ipo-stock-an-ai-robotics-startup-with-bold-claims-little
-revenue-b0c1f03b.

177   **vision-language models:** "Vision Language Models," NVIDIA, https://
www.nvidia.com/en-us/glossary/vision-language-models.

177   **an algorithm invented at OpenAI:** "CLIP: Connecting Text and Images,"
OpenAI, January 5, 2021, https://openai.com/index/clip.

178   **the first transformer-powered robot:** Vincent Vanhoucke, "Helping
Robots Learn from Each Other," Google, December 13, 2022, https://
blog.google/technology/ai/helping-robots-learn-from-each-other.

181   **Companies building cutting-edge AI:** Kylie Robison, "OpenAI Cofounder
Ilya Sutskever Says the Way AI Is Built Is About to Change," The Verge,
December 13, 2024, https://www.theverge.com/2024/12/13/24320811/
what-ilya-sutskever-sees-openai-model-data-training.

182   **the paper on the second generation:** Jorge Aldaco et al., "ALOHA 2: An
Enhanced Low-Cost Hardware for Bimanual Teleoperation," GitHub,
February 7, 2024, https://aloha-2.github.io.

12. THE MUSEUM OF ALL IDEAS

192   **EvolutionaryScale Model:** Zeming Lin et al., "Evolutionary-Scale
Prediction of Atomic-Level Protein Structure with a Language Model,"
Science 379, no. 6637 (March 16, 2023): 1123–30, https://www.science
.org/doi/10.1126/science.ade2574.

193   **improve antibodies to particular pathogens:** Prabal Chhibbar and Jishnu
Das, "Machine Learning Approaches Enable the Discovery of
Therapeutics Across Domains," *Molecular Therapy* 33, no. 5 (May 7,
2025): 2269–78, https://www.cell.com/molecular-therapy-family/
molecular-therapy/fulltext/S1525-0016(25)00275-8.

193   **a universal atlas:** James D. Pearce et al., "A Cross-Species Generative Cell
Atlas Across 1.5 Billion Years of Evolution: The TranscriptFormer
Single-Cell Model," BioRxiv, April 29, 2025, https://doi.org/10.1101/
2025.04.25.650731.

193   **predict what a newly discovered enzyme:** Gautham Dharuman et al.,
"Protein Generation via Genome-Scale Language Models with Bio-
physical Scoring," Proceedings of the SC '23 Workshops of the
International Conference on High Performance Computing,
November 12, 2023, 95–101, https://doi.org/10.1145/3624062.36260.

194   **the wildest of these fantasies:** Matteo Wong, "AI Executives Promise
Cancer Cures. Here's the Reality," *The Atlantic,* April 25, 2025, https://
www.theatlantic.com/technology/archive/2025/04/how-ai-will-actually
-contribute-cancer-cure/682607.

197   **The largest one ever characterized:** Molly Herring, "Tiny Algae Make Big

Toxins with Some of the Largest Proteins Known to Science," Science Sifter, August 9, 2024, https://www.science.org/content/article/tiny -algae-make-big-toxins-some-largest-proteins-known-science.

198   **Huang's Law:** Christopher Mims, "Huang's Law Is the New Moore's Law, and Explains Why Nvidia Wants Arm," *The Wall Street Journal,* September 19, 2020, https://www.wsj.com/articles/huangs-law-is-the -new-moores-law-and-explains-why-nvidia-wants-arm-11600488001.

201   **collectively spent close to $300 billion:** Nate Rattner and Jason Dean, "Tech Giants Double Down on Their Massive AI Spending," *The Wall Street Journal,* February 6, 2025, https://www.wsj.com/tech/ai/tech -giants-double-down-on-their-massive-ai-spending-b3040b33.

203   **a substantial improvement:** Ilan Price et al., "Probabilistic Weather Forecasting with Machine Learning," Nature, December 4, 2024, https:// www.nature.com/articles/s41586-024-08252-9.

203   **"surrogate modeling":** Elizaveta Semenova, "Case for a Unified Surrogate Modelling Framework in the Age of AI," arXiv, February 10, 2025, https://arxiv.org/html/2502.06753v1#bib.bib1.

205   **contemplated charging $20,000 a month:** Stephanie Palazzolo and Cory Weinberg, "OpenAI Plots Charging $20,000 a Month for PhD-Level Agents," The Information, March 5, 2025, https://www.theinformation .com/articles/openai-plots-charging-20-000-a-month-for-phd-level -agents.

208   **"the full automation of all work":** Julie Bort, "Famed AI Researcher Launches Controversial Startup to Replace All Human Workers Everywhere," TechCrunch, April 19, 2025, https://techcrunch.com/2025/ 04/19/famed-ai-researcher-launches-controversial-startup-to-replace-all -human-workers-everywhere.

208   **68 percent of American adults:** Colleen McClain et al., "How the U.S. Public and AI Experts View Artificial Intelligence," Pew Research Center, April 3, 2025, https://www.pewresearch.org/internet/2025/04/03/how -the-us-public-and-ai-experts-view-artificial-intelligence.

Index

Note: Page numbers in **bold** indicate definitions.

About the Author

CHRISTOPHER MIMS is a columnist who writes about technology for *The Wall Street Journal* and cohosts the *WSJ* podcast *Bold Names*. He has written about bidets, brain implants, the cult of the founder, the history of technology, innovation, venture capital, robotics, batteries, energy, materials science, wireless communications, AI, data science, telepresence, microchips, logistics, IT, 3D printing, and autonomous boats, trucks, cars, drones, and flying taxis. Mims joined the *Journal* from *Quartz*, where he also covered technology, and is the author of *Arriving Today: From Factory to Front Door—Why Everything Has Changed About How and What We Buy.*